Sadie Plant

Comment lire
a bookshelf
in einem Buch

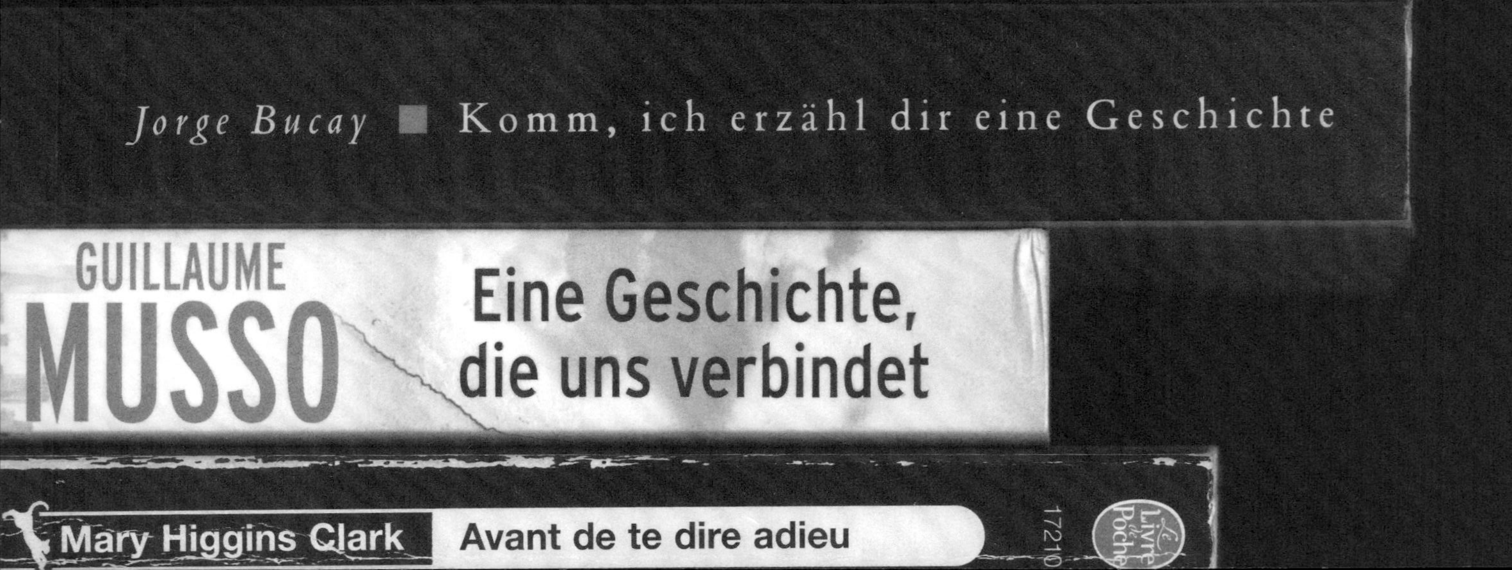

Jorge Bucay ■ Komm, ich erzähl dir eine Geschichte

GUILLAUME MUSSO

Eine Geschichte, die uns verbindet

Mary Higgins Clark Avant de te dire adieu

17210

Le Livre de Poche

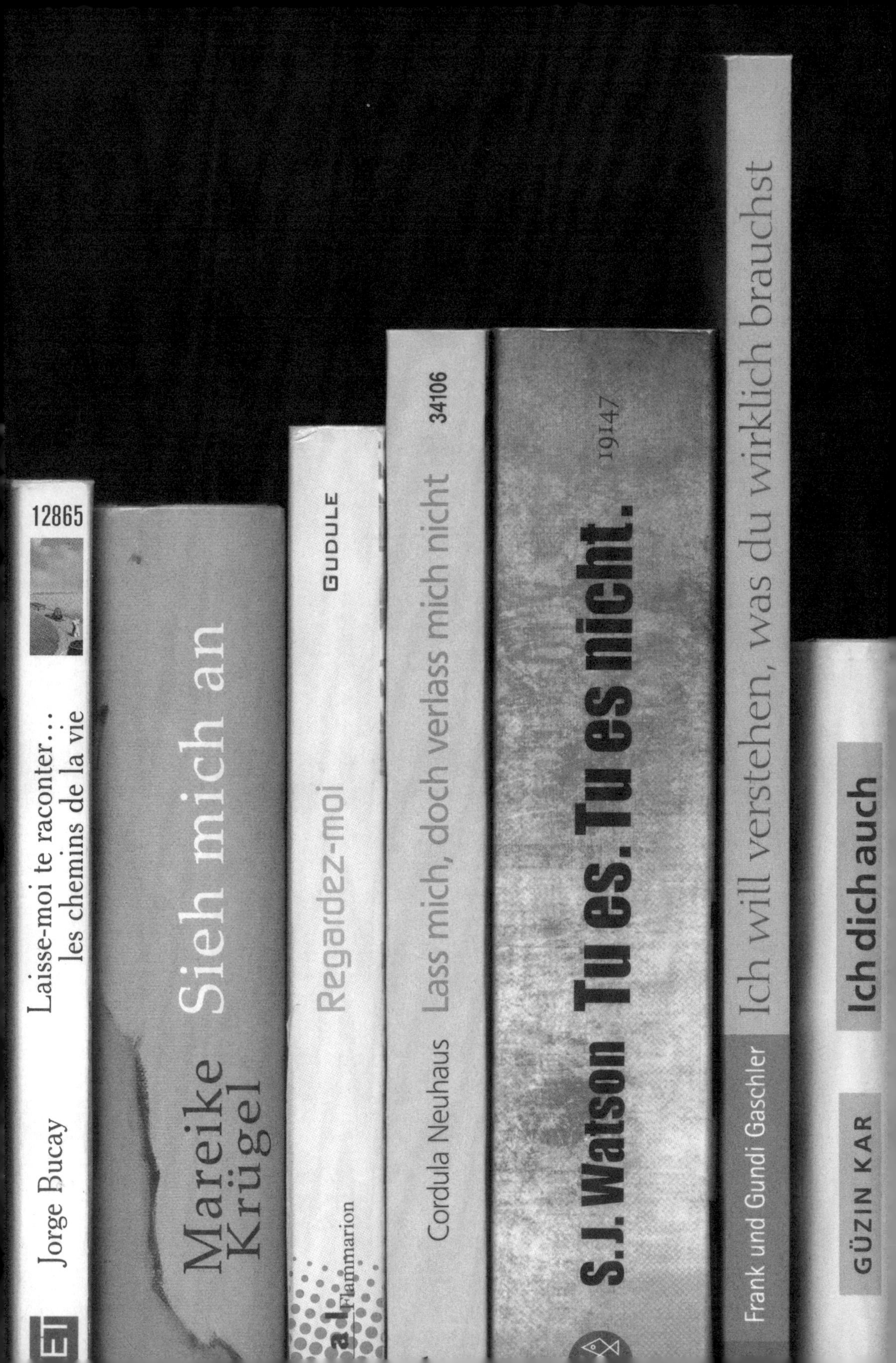

ET Jorge Bucay Laisse-moi te raconter… les chemins de la vie 12865

Mareike Krügel Sieh mich an

Flammarion Regardez-moi Gudule

Cordula Neuhaus Lass mich, doch verlass mich nicht 34106

S.J. Watson Tu es. Tu es nicht. 19147

Frank und Gundi Gaschler Ich will verstehen, was du wirklich brauchst

Güzin Kar Ich dich auch

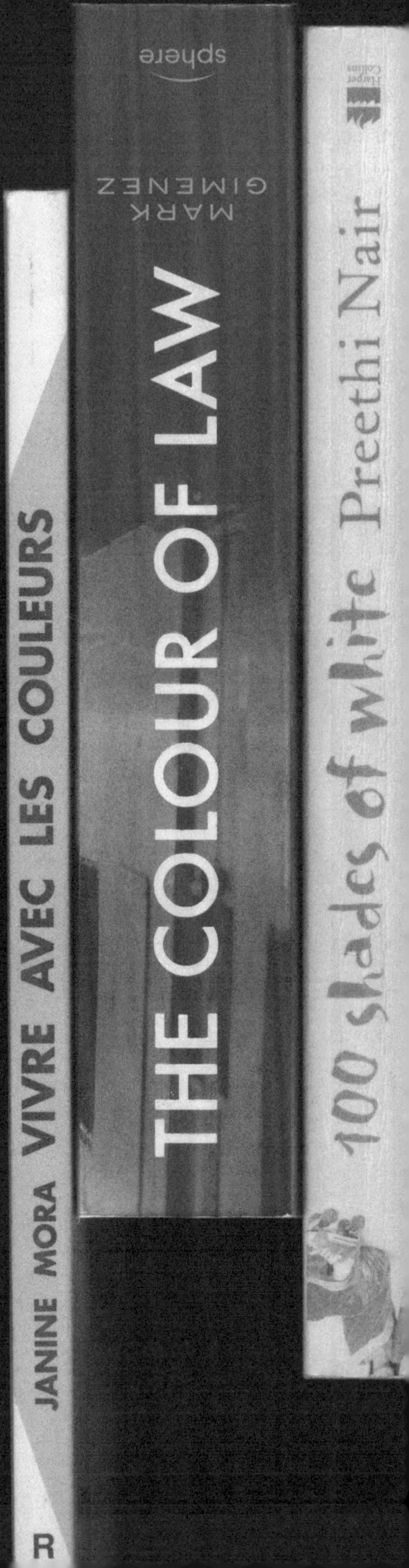

JANINE MORA VIVRE AVEC LES COULEURS
R

THE COLOUR OF LAW
MARK GIMENEZ
sphere

100 shades of white
Preethi Nair
Harper Collins

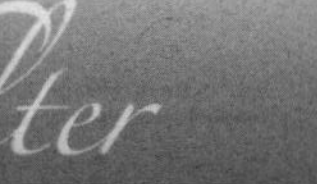
ALLA
IMUKKA
SO WEISS WIE SCHNEE
ALLA
MUKKA
SO ROT WIE BLUT
Mach's BUNT
WARNER
Indigo
SCHNEEBERGER
NEON PINK & BLUE
DAS DREIFARBENE MEER

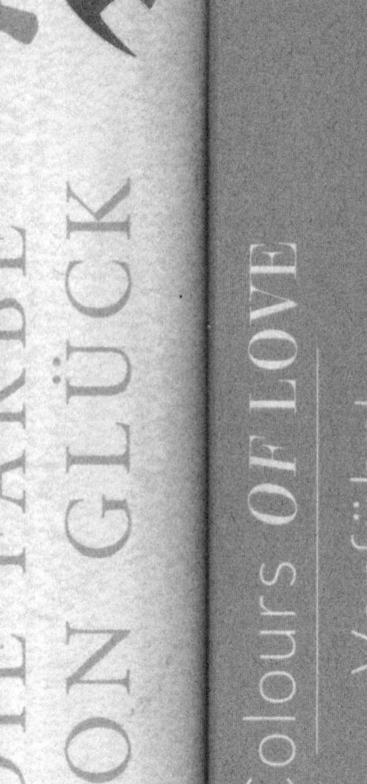
ARA MARIA
BAGUS
DIE FARBE
VON GLÜCK
thryn Taylor
Colours OF LOVE
Verführt
LA VIE EN ROUX
François Vorpe
Koningsberger
Die goldenen Schlüssel
LA SOURIS VERTE
Robert Sa
Sucre brun
NANCY CATO

List
Åke Edwardson Rotes Meer

Grasset
Metin Arditi Carnaval noir

BALLAND LE NOIR EST UNE COULEUR GRISÉLIDIS RÉAL

Jutta Treiber *Der blaue See ist heute grün*

PAM JENOFF IL COLORE TRASPARENTE DELLA NOTTE

Edizioni Comedit 2000 LA VERITÀ NON HA COLORE D. Franchi - L. Miani

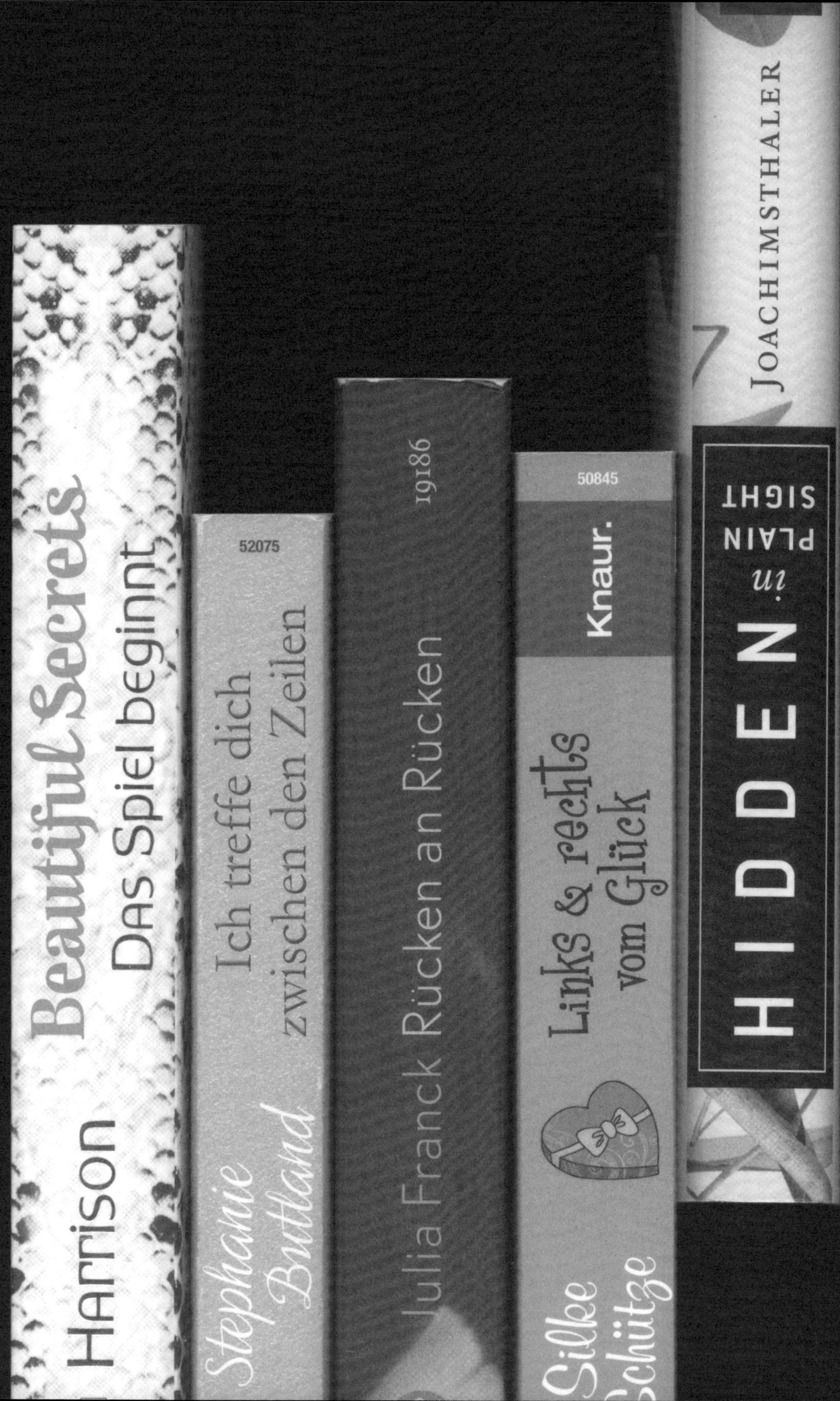

Harrison
Beautiful Secrets
Das Spiel beginnt

Stephanie Butland
Ich treffe dich zwischen den Zeilen
52075

Julia Franck Rücken an Rücken
1986

Silke Schütze
Links & rechts vom Glück
Knaur.
50845

HIDDEN in PLAIN SIGHT
JOACHIMSTHALER

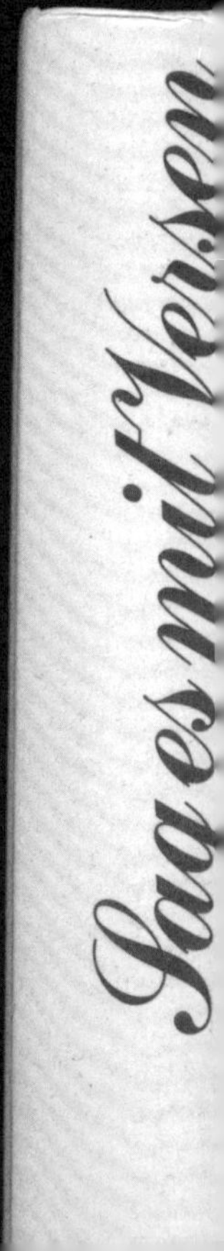

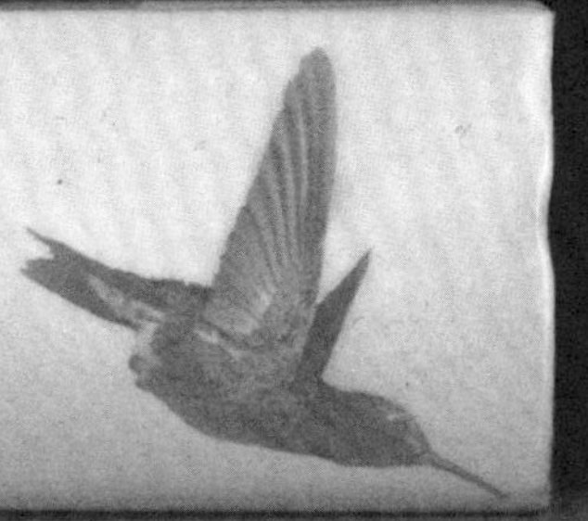
MON Gebt uns eine Chance!
VENT DESSUS, VENT DEDANS Marin-Marie
LIRE UNE IMAGE MARIE-CLAUDE VETTRAINO-SOULARD
COMMUNICATION Enseignement
TAIS-TOI ET PLONGE! CLAUDINE MOULY
Laß endlich los und lebe
Lebe, was Dich glücklich macht
eider
hapiro
DAS KANN ICH SELBST!

ahar Ben Jelloun *Papa, was ist ein Fremder?*

BEGINNER BOOKS Are You My Mother? Ea

Gabriela Zander-Schneider Sind Sie meine Tochter?

VANOTTI YO, BROTHERS AND SISTERS
Siamo o ... siamo un bel movimento?

AKUYE OYASIN "We are all related" Dr. A.C. Ross

KARA MCDOWELL ONE WAY OR ANOTHER

Noemi Schneider Das wissen wir schon 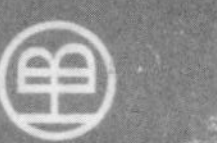

Was zeigt die Uhr?

einfach für zwei

Andrea Köhler Lange Weile

John Cage A YEAR FROM MONDAY

WESLEYAN

602

A DAY'S WORK

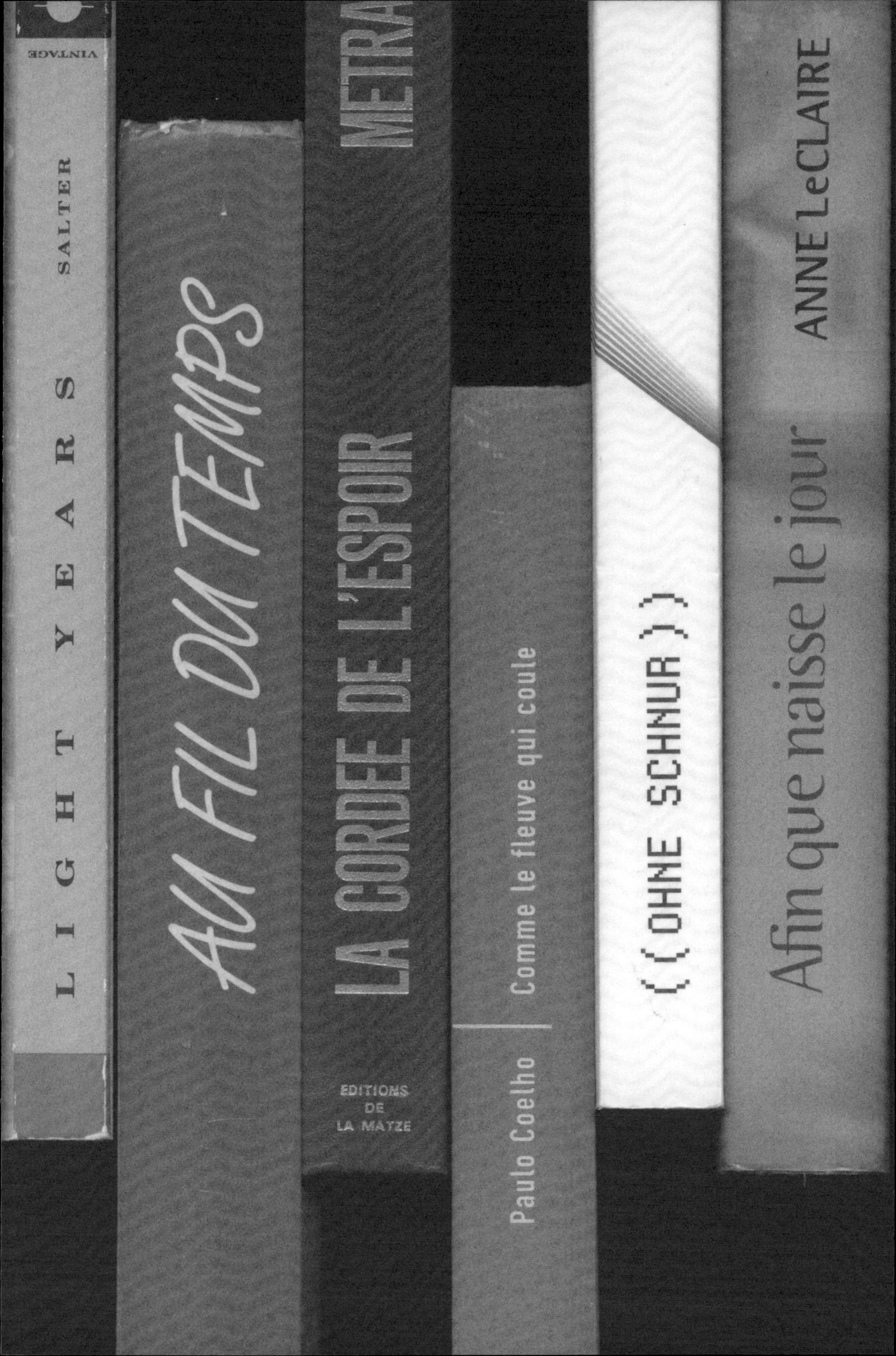

LIGHT YEARS SALTER VINTAGE

AU FIL DU TEMPS

EDITIONS DE LA MATZE LA CORDEE DE L'ESPOIR METRA

Paulo Coelho | Comme le fleuve qui coule

((OHNE SCHNUR))

Afin que naisse le jour ANNE LeCLAIRE

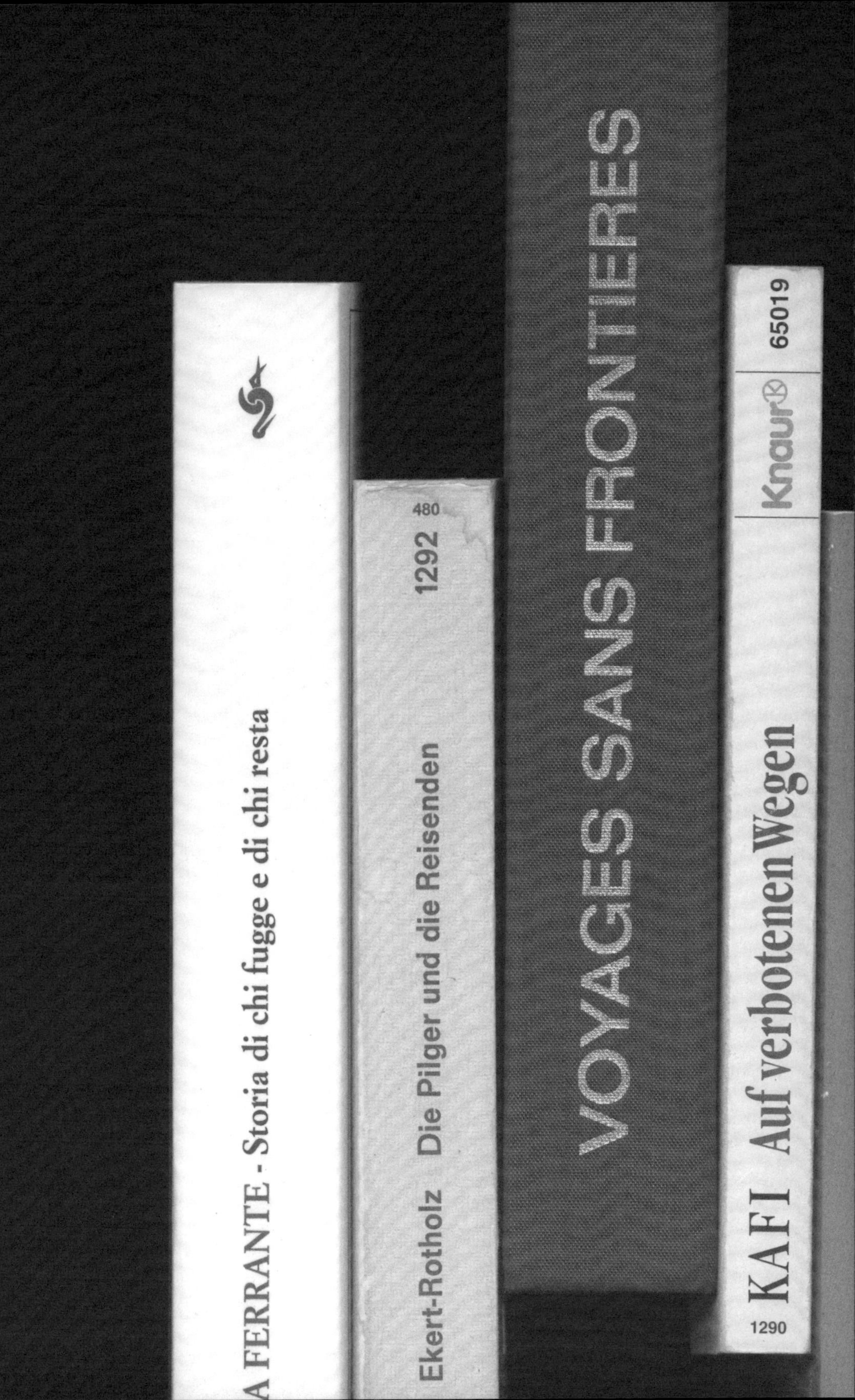

A FERRANTE - Storia di chi fugge e di chi resta

Ekert-Rotholz Die Pilger und die Reisenden 1292 480

VOYAGES SANS FRONTIERES

1290 KAFI Auf verbotenen Wegen Knaur 65019

CONNELLY JUSQU'À L'IMPENSABLE
SOCIÉTÉ
DES EXPLORATEURS
FRANÇAIS
CLAUDE COLLIN DELAVAUD
JUSQU'AU BOUT DE LA TERRE

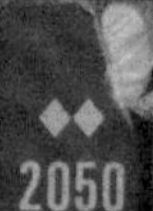

2050
KONSALIK
JUSQU'AU BOUT DE L'AMOUR

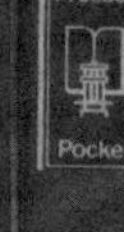

Presses
Pocket
15759

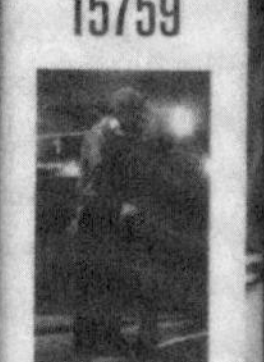

Pour un jour avec toi
Forman

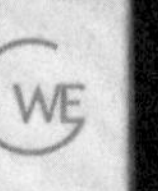
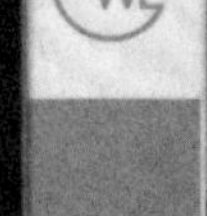

WE
VENISE 2013
Un Grand Week-end

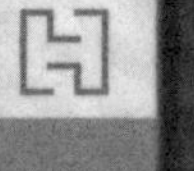
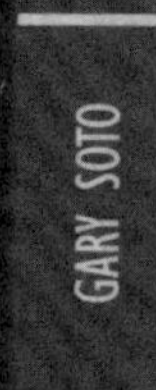

562
GARY SOTO
UN WEEK-END FOU
Flammarion
CASTOR POCHE
15711
RSTIN GIER Ach, wär ich nur zu Hause geblieb
Michel Layaz
Die fröhliche Moritat von der Bleibe

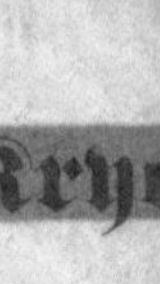

Kryo
Die Reise nach Hause

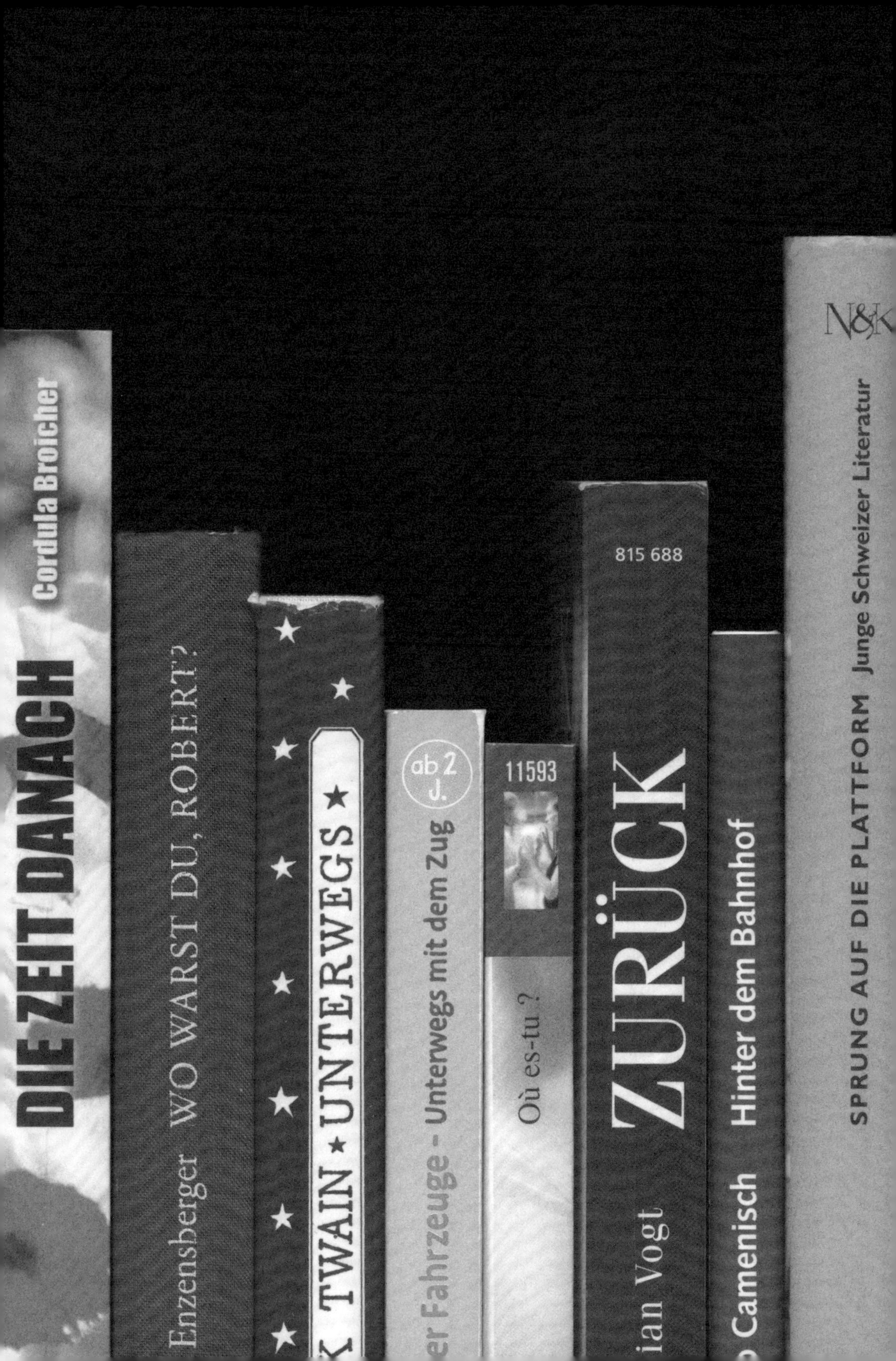

Cordula Broicher DIE ZEIT DANACH

Enzensberger WO WARST DU, ROBERT?

TWAIN ★ UNTERWEGS ★

ab 2 J.
er Fahrzeuge - Unterwegs mit dem Zug

11593
Où es-tu ?

815 688
ian Vogt ZURÜCK

Camenisch Hinter dem Bahnhof

N&K
SPRUNG AUF DIE PLATTFORM Junge Schweizer Literatur

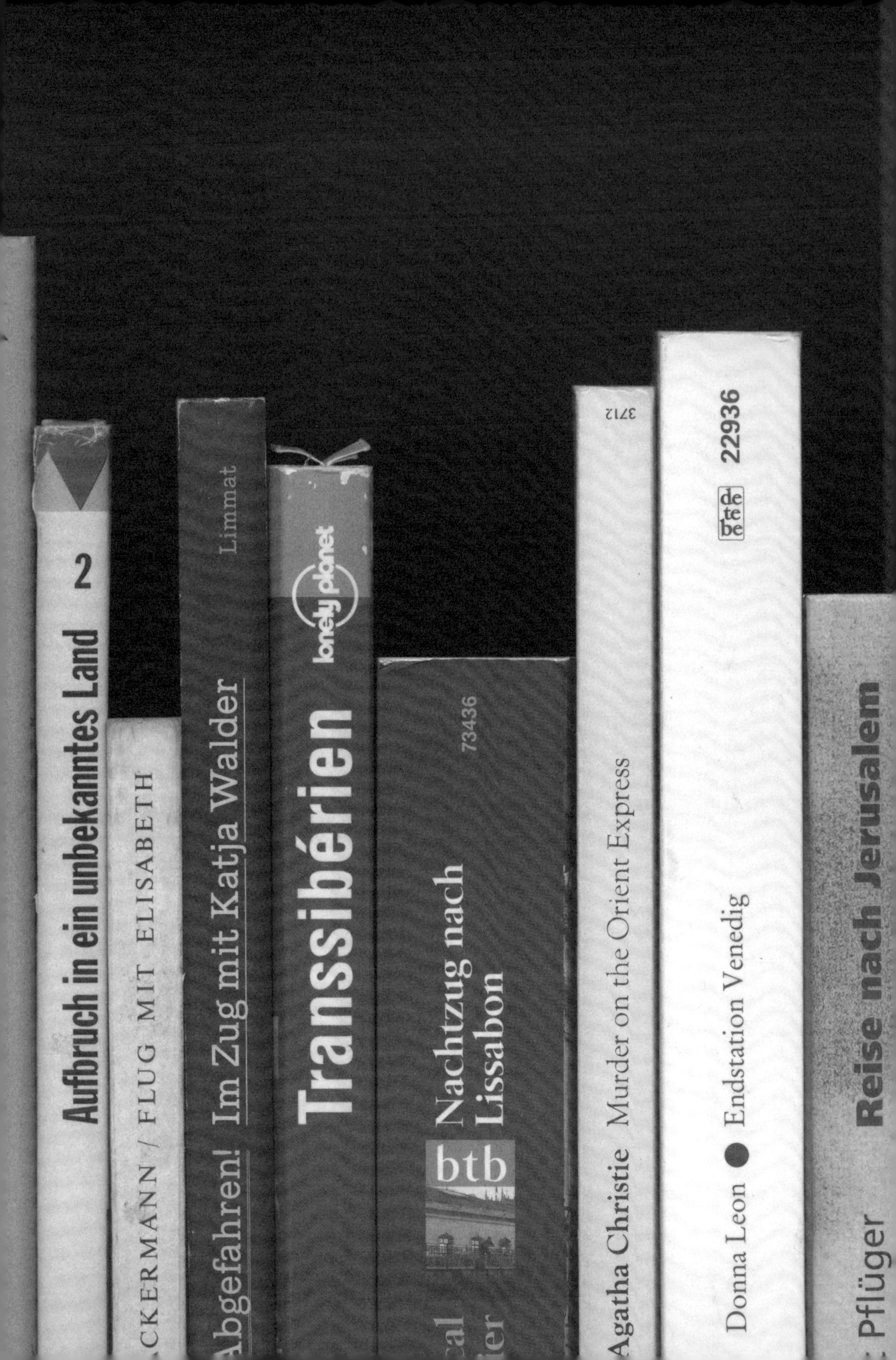

Aufbruch in ein unbekanntes Land 2

CKERMANN / FLUG MIT ELISABETH

Abgefahren! Im Zug mit Katja Walder Limmat

Transsibérien lonely planet

cal
er
btb Nachtzug nach Lissabon 73436

Agatha Christie Murder on the Orient Express 3712

Donna Leon ● Endstation Venedig dtebe 22936

Pflüger Reise nach Jerusalem

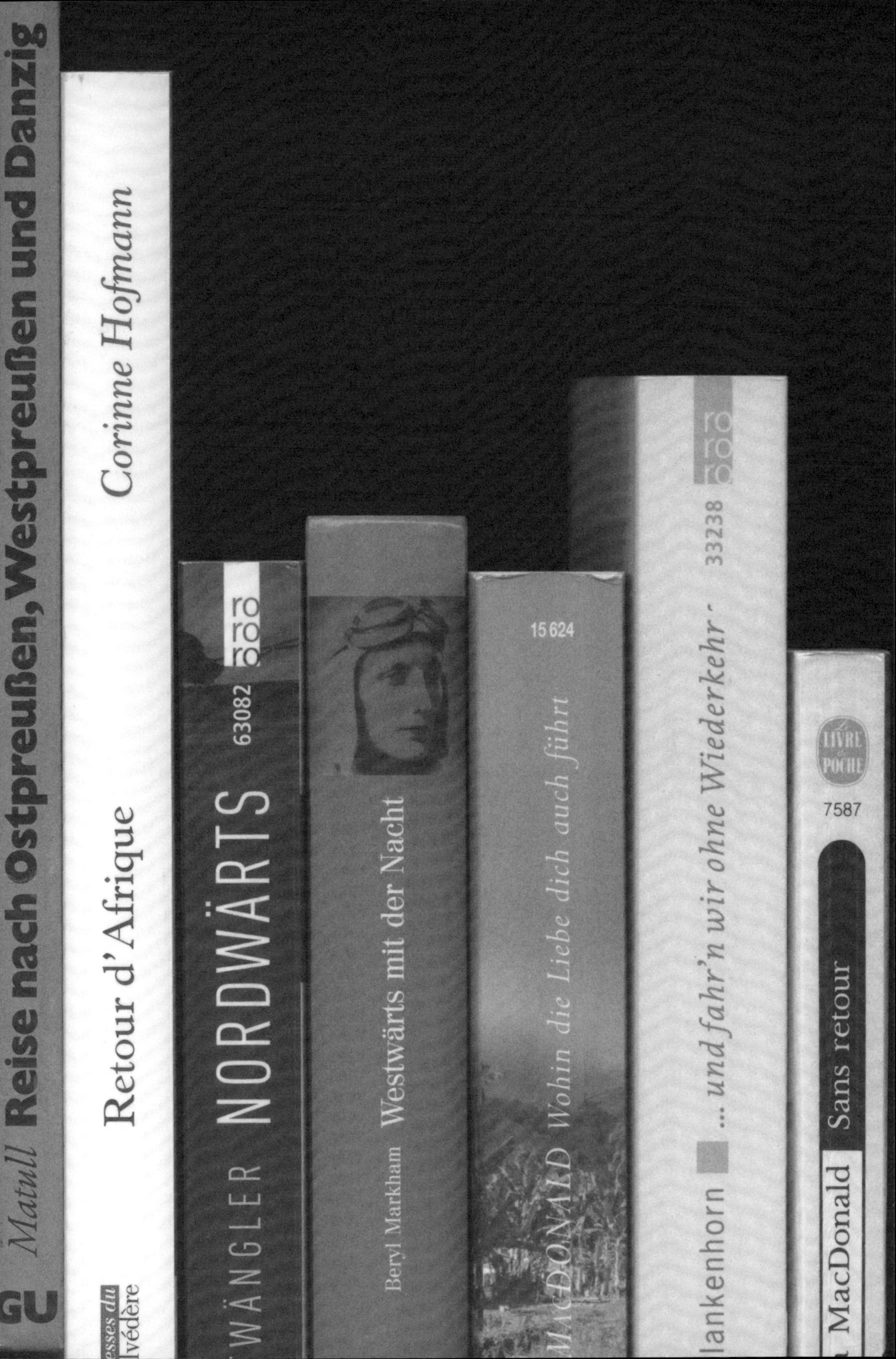

GU Matull Reise nach Ostpreußen, Westpreußen und Danzig

esses du lvédère Retour d'Afrique Corinne Hofmann

WÄNGLER NORDWÄRTS 63082 rororo

Beryl Markham Westwärts mit der Nacht

MACDONALD Wohin die Liebe dich auch führt 15 624

lankenhorn ... und fahr'n wir ohne Wiederkehr 33238 rororo

MacDonald Sans retour 7587 LIVRE DE POCHE

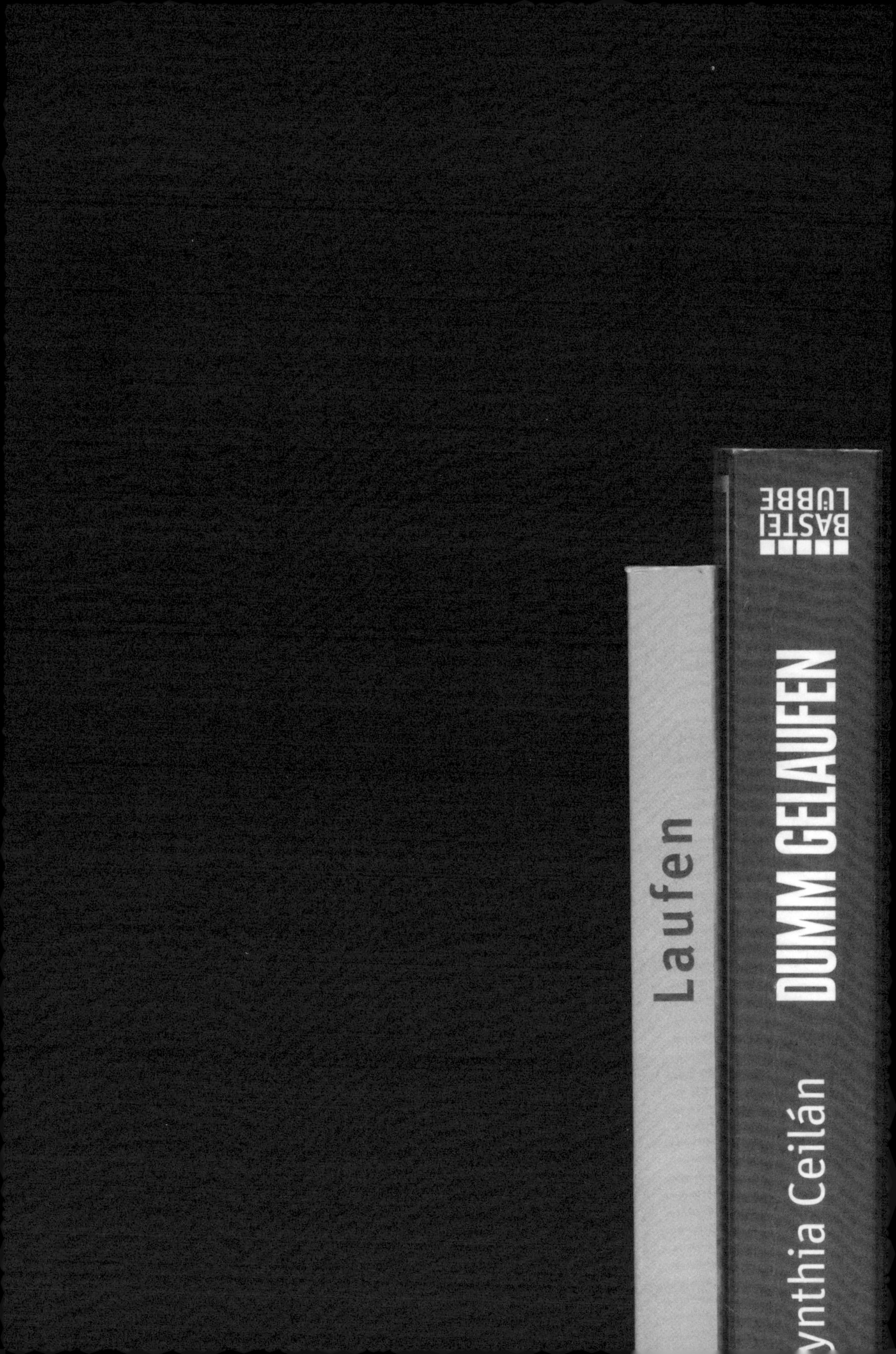

BASTEI LÜBBE

DUMM GELAUFEN

ynthia Ceilán

Laufen

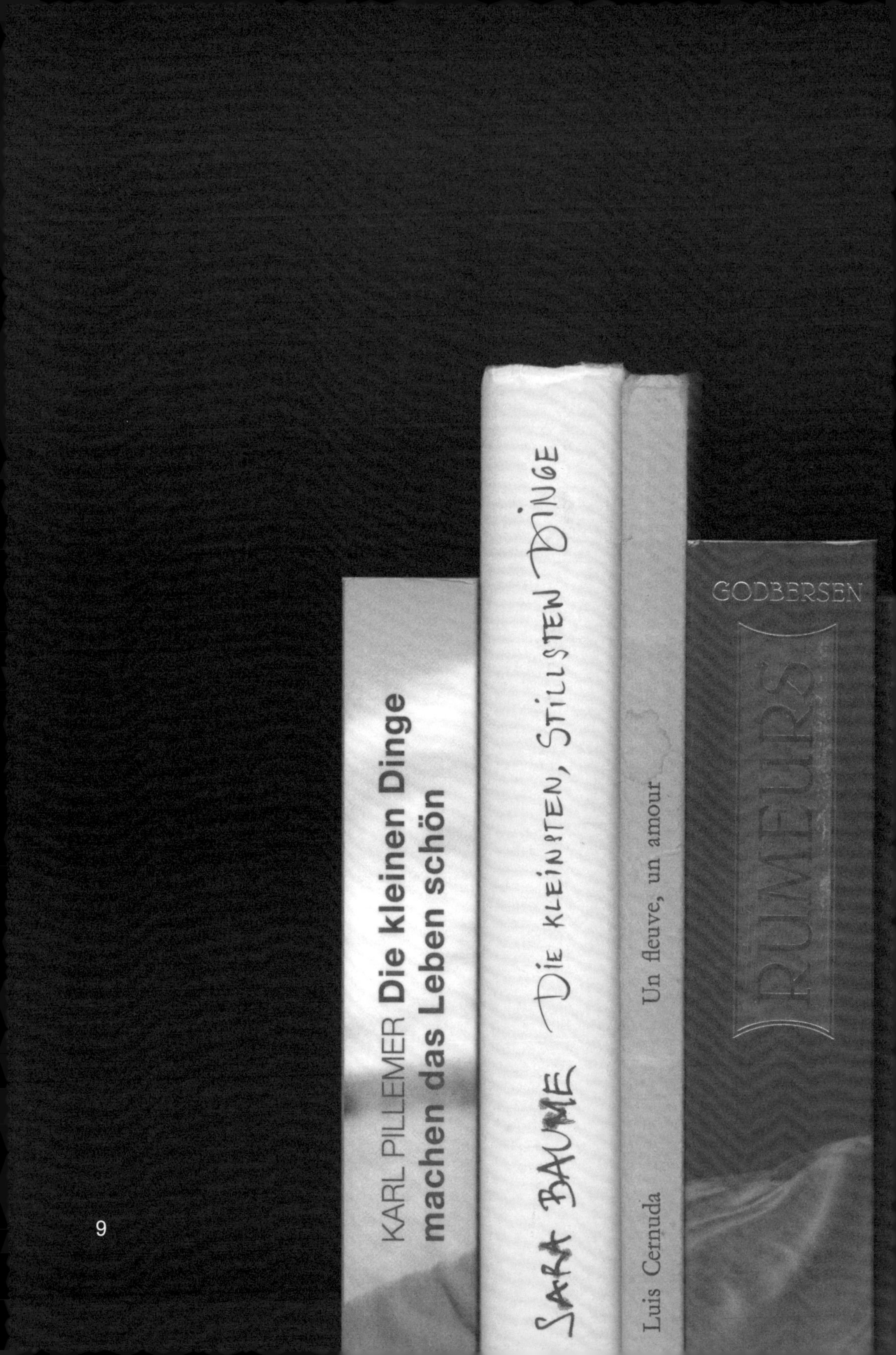

KARL PILLEMER Die kleinen Dinge machen das Leben schön

SARA BAUME DIE KLEINSTEN, STILLSTEN DINGE

Luis Cernuda Un fleuve, un amour

GODBERSEN RUMEURS

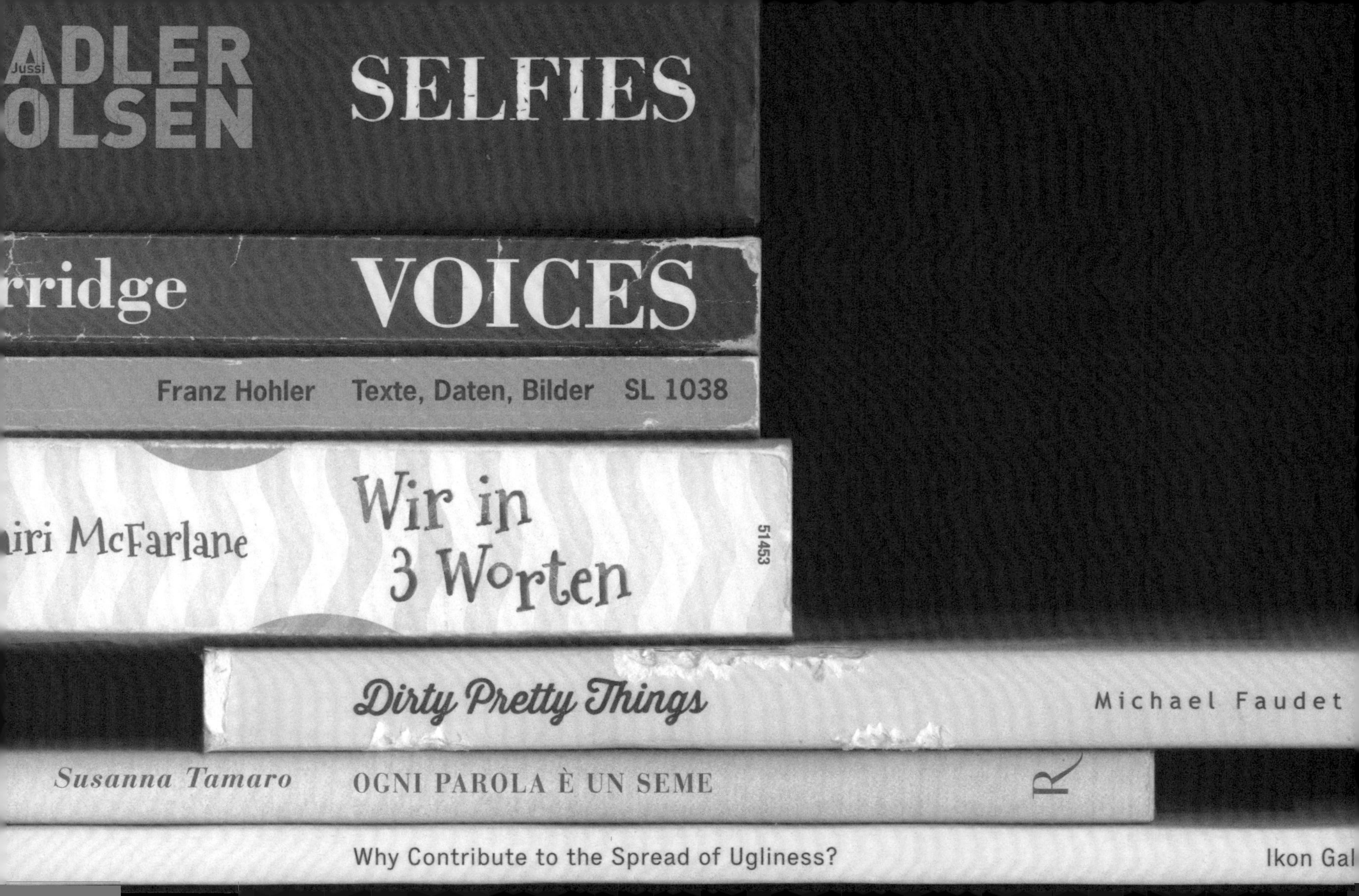

Jussi ADLER OLSEN SELFIES

rridge VOICES

Franz Hohler Texte, Daten, Bilder SL 1038

iri McFarlane Wir in 3 Worten 51453

Dirty Pretty Things Michael Faudet

Susanna Tamaro OGNI PAROLA È UN SEME R

Why Contribute to the Spread of Ugliness? Ikon Gal

LE LIBRERIE E LO STUDIO

DR JEKYLL AND MR HYDE Robert Louis Stevenson OXFORD

Jacques Monod Le hasard et la nécessité Points

GRIMM/BERNADETTE Der Wolf und die sieben jungen Geisslein

Michel Bory LE BARBARE ET LES JONQUILLES

Vargas Llosa La tante Julia et le scribouillard 1649

La carte et le territoire — Michel Houellebecq

P. SARTRE • LE DIABLE ET LE BON DIEU

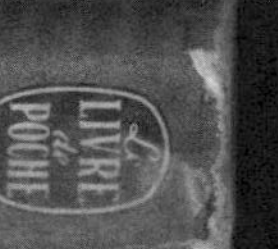

Jane Austen Stolz und Vorurteil 12350

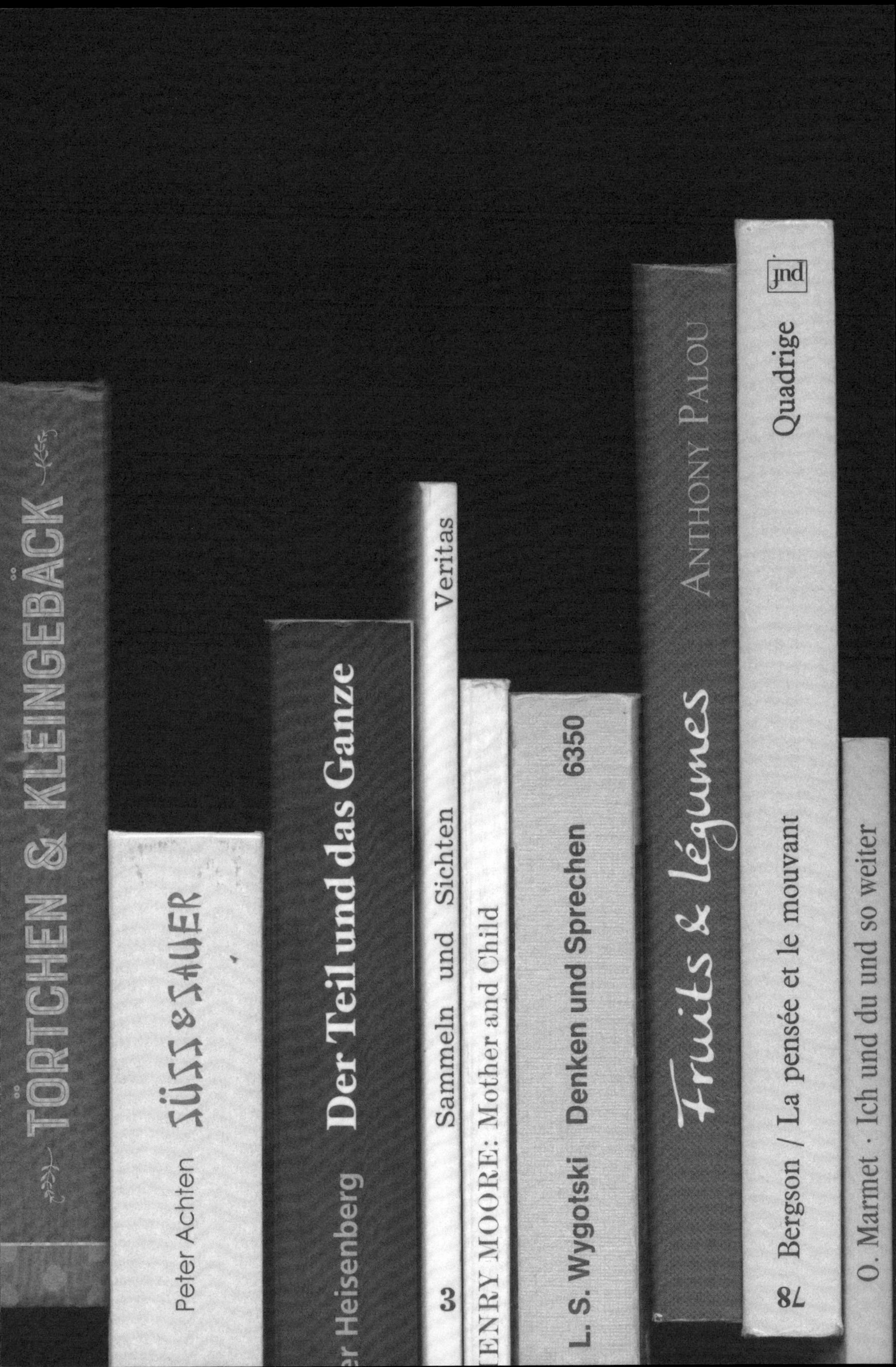

TÖRTCHEN & KLEINGEBÄCK

Peter Achten SÜSS & SAUER

er Heisenberg Der Teil und das Ganze

3 Sammeln und Sichten Veritas

ENRY MOORE: Mother and Child

L. S. Wygotski Denken und Sprechen 6350

Fruits & légumes ANTHONY PALOU

78 Bergson / La pensée et le mouvant Quadrige puf

O. Marmet · Ich und du und so weiter

Dirk von Nayhauß 7 Fragen an das Leben
Wiebke Lorenz Was? Wäre? Wenn?
ar · Peter Gut Wer ist der Größte?
Wo kommt das her?
P. LANARES QUI DOMINERA LE MONDE?
Landa • Warum wackeln Wolkenkratzer?
I Used to Know That GEOGRAPHY WILL WILLIAMS

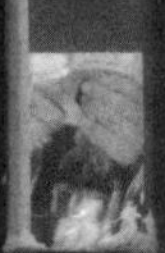

TASTE AND OTHER TALES

Roald Dahl

LONGMAN

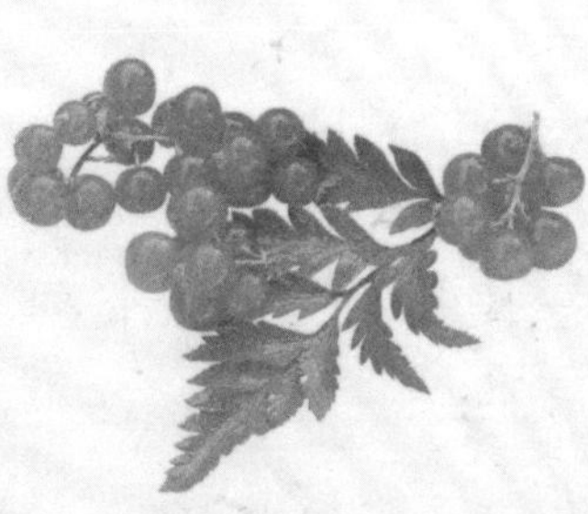

SAVEURS

d'hier & d'aujourd'hui

Patrick Süskind ● Das Parfum

de te be

22800

Robert Walser Die Rose

ALL
Dolce Yasmine

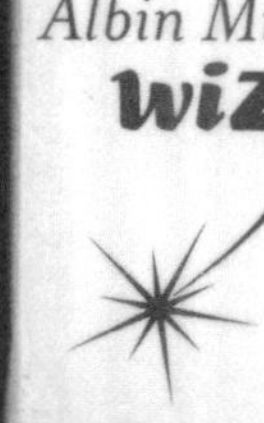

Albin Michel
wiz
Peau de pêche
j.l. anderson

Mirjam Pressler
Bitterschokolade
1103

dtv
1990
Ryan
Ich bin so wild nach Kirschsorbet
36074

HEYNE
680
Klaus Kinski
ICH BIN SO WILD NACH DEINEM ERDBEERMUND
5382

"HELLO MY BIG BIG HONEY!"
Dave Walker and Richard S. Ehrlic

Souviens-toi
MARY HIGGINS CLARK

مرسم
MARSAM
Le Jardin des Amoureux
Fat

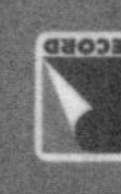
UNBERECHENBAR
Fiquei com o seu número

Kristina Ohlsson TAUSENDSCHÖN 37581 blanvalet

emons: 111 LIEUX À BIENNE 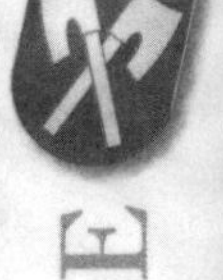 À NE PAS MANQUER

BALDWIN · HUNDERT JAHRE FREIHEIT 634

c Beigbeder 99 francs 4062

vanagh FIFTY FIFTY 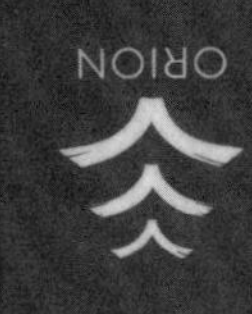 ORION

Maugham: Eine Frau von fünfzig Jahren 25013

CRACE QUARANTINE 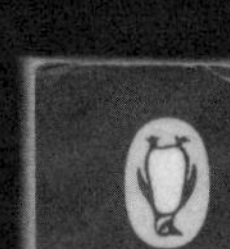 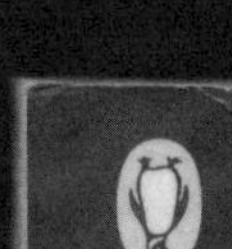

D/ SOLIN VINGT DÉFIS POUR LA PLANÈTE... J.-F. RISCHARD

18254
13 à table !
2021

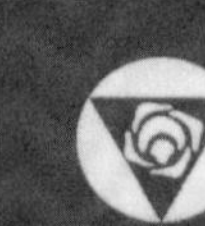
Die zwölf wilden Schwäne
wk &
ary Valentine

Christian Poslaniec La onzième souris verte

Daniel de Roulet Dix Petites Anarchistes

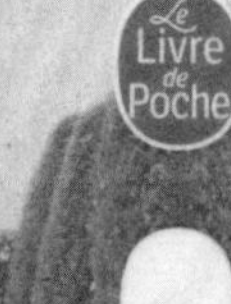

LIANE MORIARTY
NEUF PARFAITS ÉTRANGERS

10344
ACHT BERGE
O
TTI

KAREN GILLECE
Sieben Tage, sieben Nächte

Cinq Galops de Chevaux

FOUR QUARTETS T. S. ELIOT

Drei Schritte

DEUX CHATS *sous* UN MÊME TOIT PATTI DAVIS

Eindeutig zweideutig

anovich *Einmal ist keinmal* 42877

ZEROS + ONES SADIE PLANT

Bret Easton Ellis – Moins que zéro 1914

itali Di impossibile non c'è niente

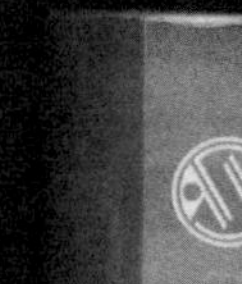

oherty Cher inconnu Scripto

MARION GOEDELT WO BIST DU ZU HAUSE?

ABOLO MBUE Das geträumte LAND

Utta Danella · Niemandsland

77107

étrey-Savary BORDERLINE

EDITIONS D'EN BAS

Edouard MICHEL

SANS DOMICILE FIXE

BERT PARIS - Envoyé spécial CLANDESTINO

AUREL

RIA NUROWSKA Dein Name geht dir voraus

24635

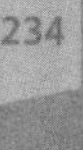

CARLSEN Dies ist KEIN REISEFÜHRER

KLIMA

THRIFTBOOKS
626
07 23406 626

COLLAPSE Philosophical Research and Development VOLUM
ax Huwyler De Wind hed gcheert

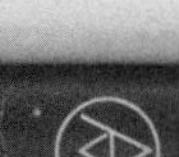

RADIKALE VERÄNDERUNGEN STEHEN BEVOR DR. HANS HEINZ
100 Dinge, die man diesen Sommer gemacht haben sollte.
Presses KONSALIK UN ÉTÉ PAS COMME LES AUTRES 1885
Boris Pasternak The Last Summer 1547
Hutter/Catherine Louis Mamma mia! was haben wir geweint
Le Déluge
Mark Twight Steig oder stirb SERIE PIPER 4864
WAS TUN, WENN'S BRENNT? Knaur 61965

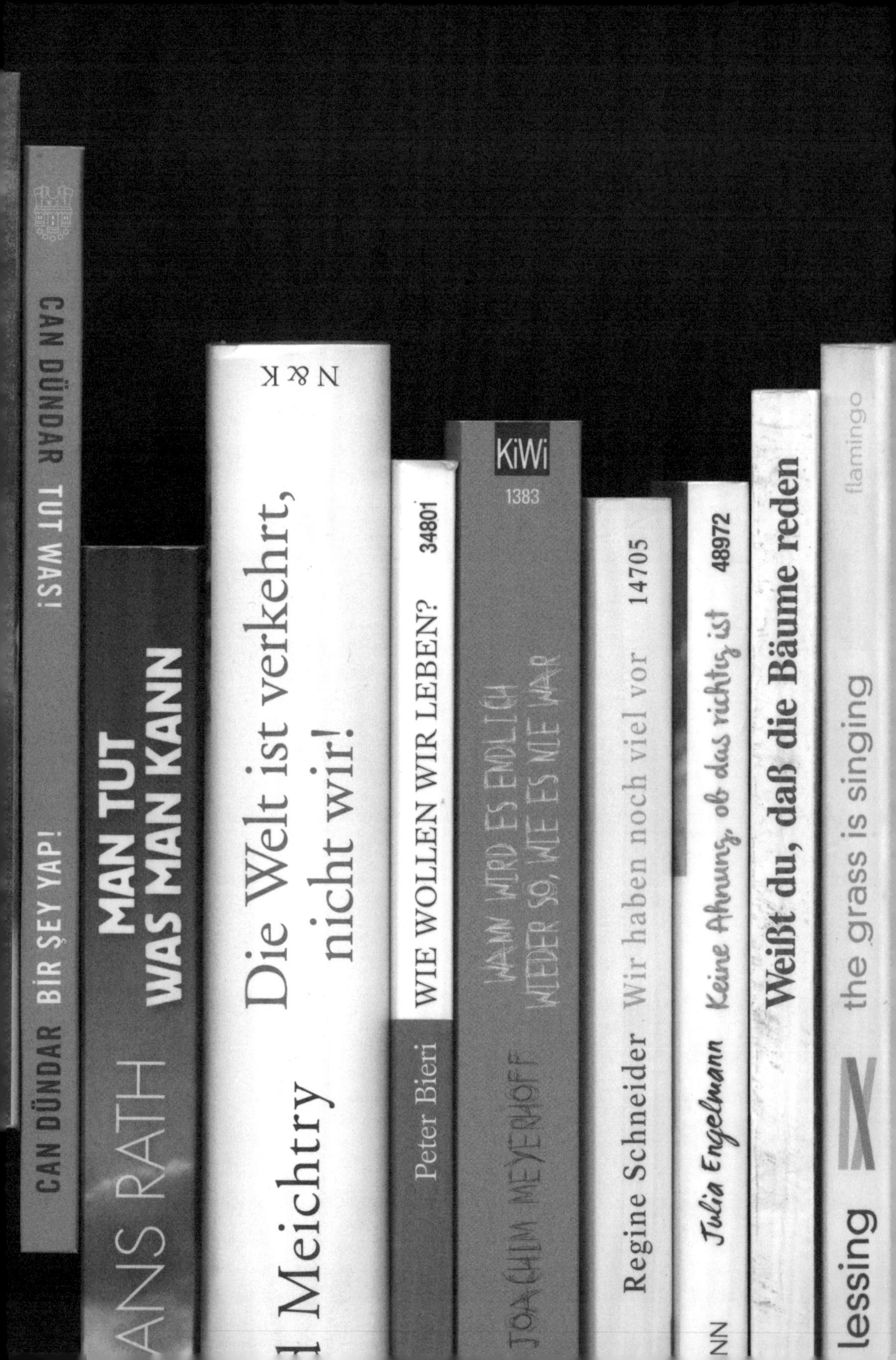

CAN DÜNDAR BİR ŞEY YAP! CAN DÜNDAR TUT WAS!

ANS RATH MAN TUT WAS MAN KANN

l Meichtry Die Welt ist verkehrt, nicht wir! N & K

Peter Bieri WIE WOLLEN WIR LEBEN? 34801

JOACHIM MEYERHOFF WANN WIRD ES ENDLICH WIEDER SO, WIE ES NIE WAR 1383 KiWi

Regine Schneider Wir haben noch viel vor 14705

NN Julia Engelmann Keine Ahnung, ob das richtig ist 48972

Weißt du, daß die Bäume reden

lessing the grass is singing flamingo

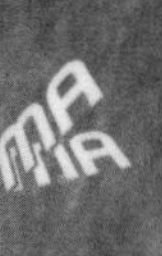

LE CHANT DES ABEILLES

JACQUELINE FREEMAN

À l'écoute

Nicky Kinnaird

HAYMON

Geoffrey Ball

... und ich höre doch!

Faltner · DIE ERDE LIEBT UNS

Anna Gavalda

Ich habe sie geliebt

15803

DOUGLAS ADAMS
MARK CARWARDINE

Die Letzten ihrer Art

HEYNE

06115

nningham

TERRA, AR, FOGO E ÁGUA

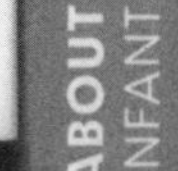

12789

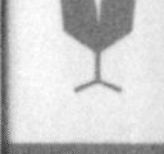

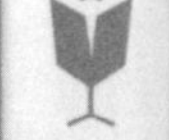

J'AI LU

Jamaiplu

JOSIANE BALASKO

POCHE MARABOUT
ENFANT

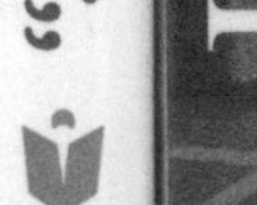

"J'ai tout essayé !"

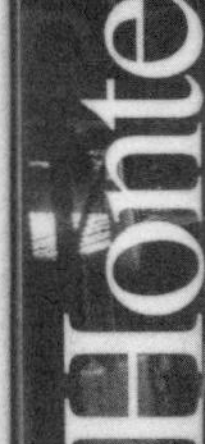

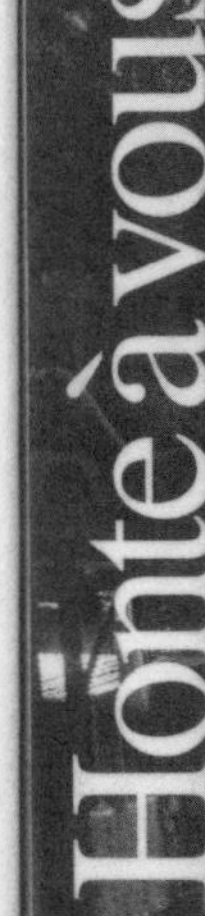

Honte à vous !

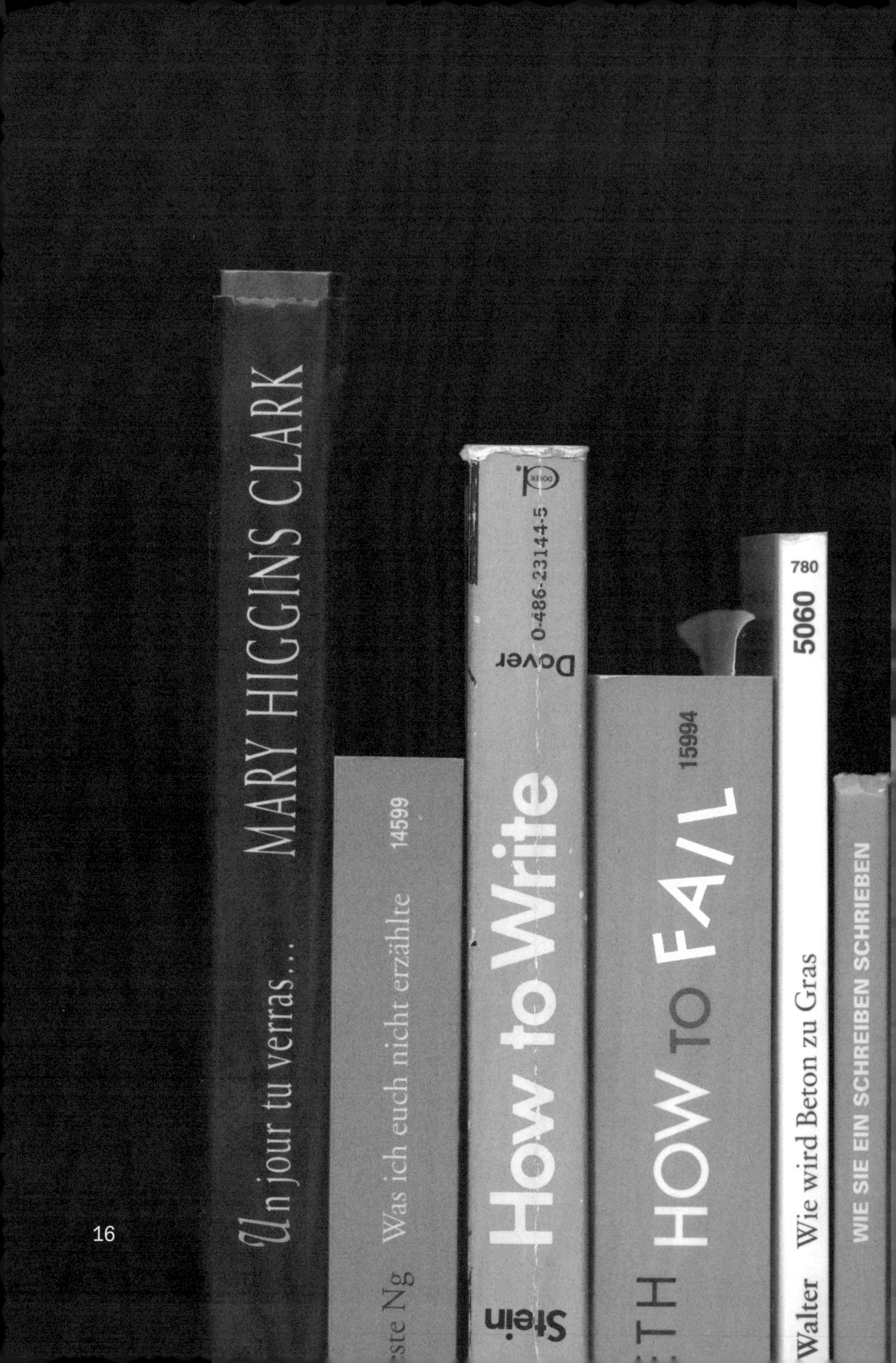

Un jour tu verras . . .   MARY HIGGINS CLARK

Celeste Ng   Was ich euch nicht erzählte   14599

Stein   How to Write   Dover   0-486-23144-5

TH   HOW TO FAIL   15994

Walter   Wie wird Beton zu Gras   5060   780

WIE SIE EIN SCHREIBEN SCHRIEBEN

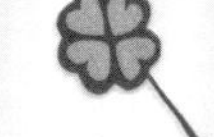
WIE EIN BLATT IM HERBSTWIND
164
WIE MAN ES VERMASSELT
Comment chier dans les bois
COMMENT DEVENIR MAÎTRE DU MONDE EN 26 LEÇONS ET DEMIE
DAN GUTMAN
Bayard JEUNESSE
WIE MAN SICH DIE WELT ERLEBT
KUNSTMANN
WIE DIE LILIEN AUF DEM FELDE
T.C. McLuhan ...WIE DER HAUCH EINES BÜFFELS IM WINTER
WIE ALLES FUNKTIONIERT
Das hätt' ich vorher wissen müssen
EVELYN SANDERS
8277

17

Randy Pausch LAST LECTURE 47137

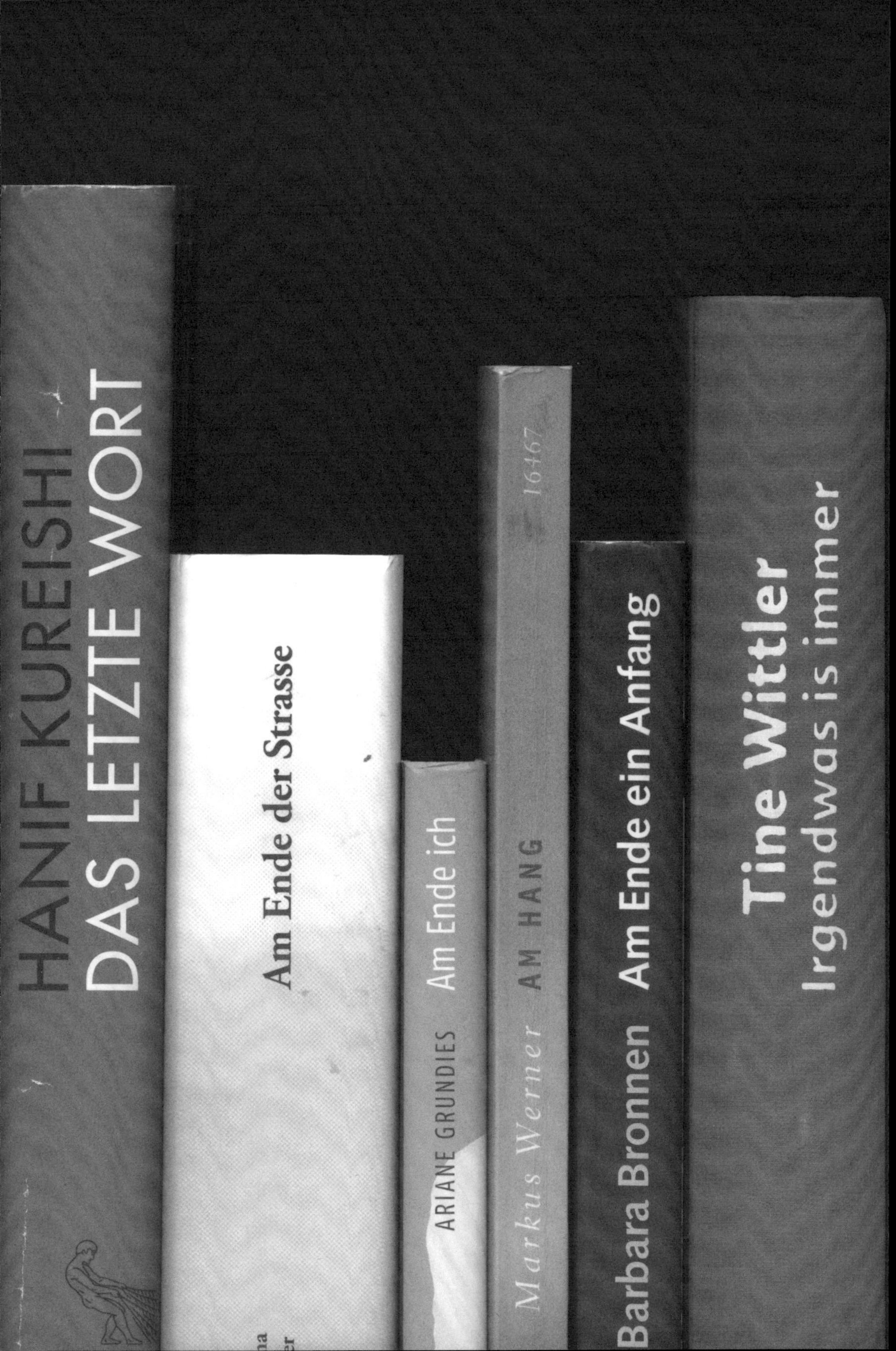

HANIF KUREISHI
DAS LETZTE WORT

Am Ende der Strasse

ARIANE GRUNDIES Am Ende ich

Markus Werner AM HANG 16467

Barbara Bronnen Am Ende ein Anfang

Tine Wittler
Irgendwas is immer

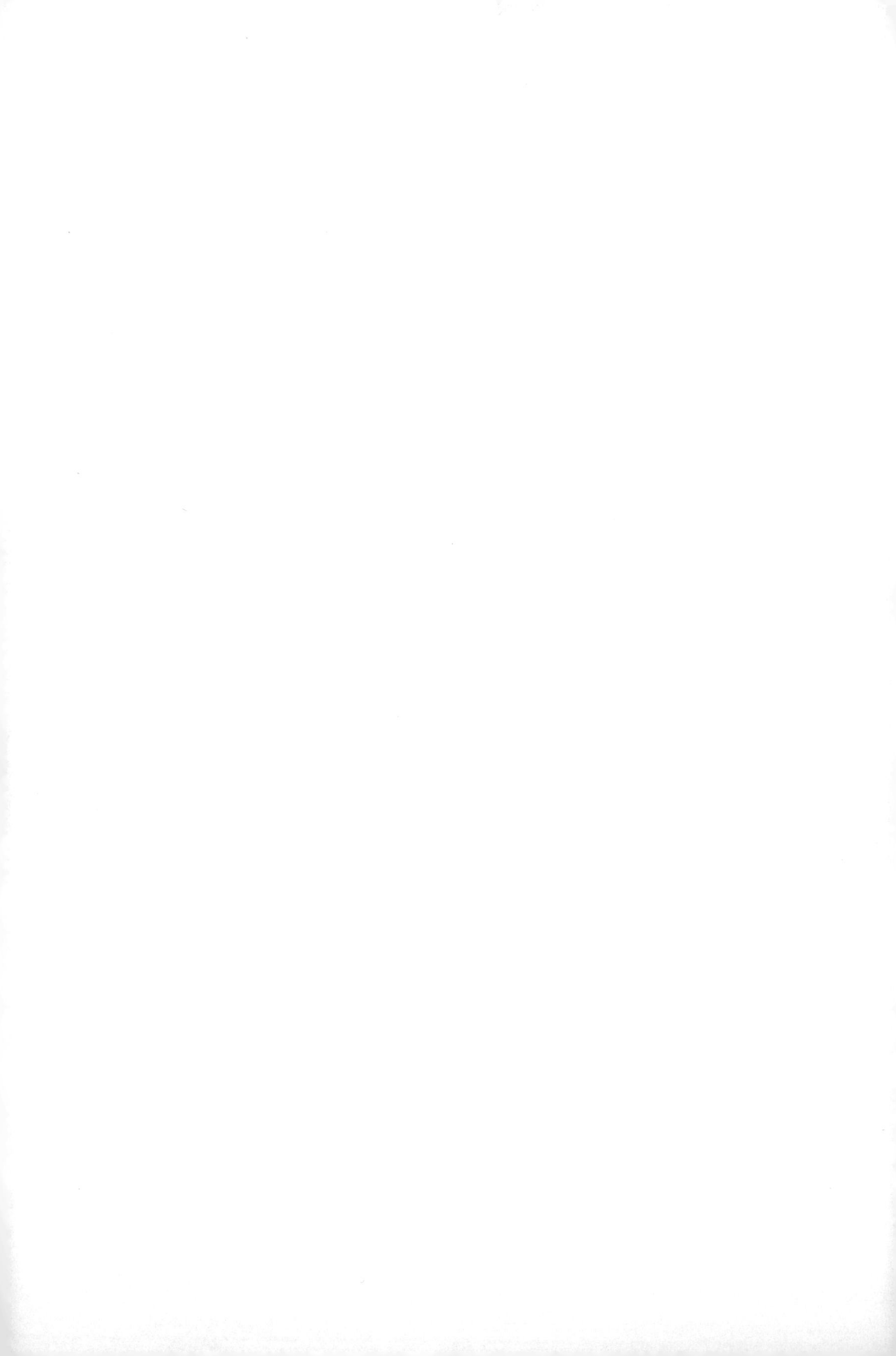

Comment lire a bookshelf in einem Buch began not as one, but many books. They were laid out on shelves in what had once been a telephone booth in a busy part of Biel/Bienne, a city in the west of Switzerland. At first sight the installation, *Comment lire a bookshelf in zwei Teilen*, looked like the kind of place in which books can be left and taken for free. But the door was locked and the books were displayed in several piles, each of which was carefully arranged so that the titles on the spines became lines of poetry.

This was writing as a physical activity: moving blocks of text around, always on the lookout for a resonance or rhyme, the right ending, the next line. The books were of all sorts: literary classics, recipes, comics, children's stories, self-help guides, pulp fiction paperbacks, full colour coffee table books, whatever came to hand. One or two I took from my own shelves; most were found in precisely the kind of places in which books are left to be taken away, surplus to the requirements of the digital age.

In *Comment lire a bookshelf in einem Buch*, these compilations are compiled again; the books that became poems now become a book that celebrates all the poems that are not completely hidden, but are yet to be seen.

Sadie Plant

1 **Komm, ich erzähl dir eine Geschichte**
Eine Geschichte
Die uns verbindet
Avant de te dire adieu
Laisse-moi te raconter...
Les chemins de la vie
Sieh mich an
Regardez-moi
Lass mich, doch verlass mich nicht
Tu es. Tu es nicht.
Ich will verstehen
Was du wirklich brauchst
Ich dich auch

2 **Vivre avec les couleurs**
The colour of law
100 shades of white
So weiss wie Schnee
So rot wie Blut
Mach's bunt
Indigo
Neon pink & blue
Das dreifarbene Meer
Die Farbe von Glück
Colours of love
La vie en roux
Die goldenen Schlüssel
La souris verte
Sucre brun
Rotes Meer
Carnaval noir
Le noir est une couleur
Der blaue See ist heute grün
Il colore trasparente della notte
La verità non ha colore

3 **Beautiful secrets**
Das Spiel beginnt
Ich treffe dich zwischen den Zeilen
Rücken an Rücken
Links & rechts vom Glück
Hidden in plain sight

4 **Sag es mit Versen**
Gebt uns eine Chance!
Vent dessus, vent dedans
Lire une image
Tais-toi et plonge !
Lass endlich los und lebe
Lebe, was Dich glücklich macht
Das kann ich selbst!

5 **Papa, was ist ein Fremder?**
Are you my mother?
Sind Sie meine Tochter?
Yo, brothers and sisters
We are all related
One way or another
Das wissen wir schon

6 **Was zeigt die Uhr?**
Einfach für zwei
Lange Weile
A year from Monday
A day's work
Light years
Au fil du temps
La cordée de l'espoir
Comme le fleuve qui coule
Ohne Schnur
Afin que naisse le jour

7 **Storia di chi fugge e di chi resta**
Die Pilger und die Reisenden
Voyages sans frontières
Auf verbotenen Wegen
Jusqu'à l'impensable
Jusqu'au bout de la terre
Jusqu'au bout de l'amour
Pour un jour avec toi
Un grand week-end
Un week-end fou
Ach, wär ich nur zu Hause geblieben
Die fröhliche Moritat von der Bleibe
Die Reise nach Hause
Die Zeit danach
Wo warst du, Robert?
Unterwegs
Unterwegs mit dem Zug
Où es-tu ?
Zurück
Hinter dem Bahnhof
Sprung auf die Plattform
Aufbruch in ein unbekanntes Land
Flug mit Elisabeth
Im Zug mit Katja Walder
Transsibérien
Nachtzug nach Lissabon
Murder on the Orient Express
Endstation Venedig
Reise nach Jerusalem
Reise nach Ostpreussen, Westpreussen und Danzig
Retour d'Afrique
Nordwärts
Westwärts mit der Nacht
Wohin die Liebe dich auch führt
... und fahr'n wir ohne Wiederkehr
Sans retour

8 **Laufen**
Dumm Gelaufen

9 **Die kleinen Dinge machen das Leben schön**
Die kleinsten, stillsten Dinge
Un fleuve, un amour
Rumeurs
Selfies
Voices
Texte, Daten, Bilder
Wir in 3 Worten
Dirty pretty things
Ogni parola è un seme
Why contribute to the spread of ugliness?

10 **Le librerie e lo studio**
Dr Jekyll and Mr Hyde
Le hasard et la nécessité
Der Wolf und die sieben jungen Geisslein
Le barbare et les jonquilles
La tante Julia et le scribouillard
La carte et la territoire
Le Diable et le bon Dieu
Stolz und Vorurteil
Törtchen & Kleingebäck
Süss & Sauer
Der Teil und das Ganze
Sammeln und sichten
Mother and child
Denken und sprechen
Fruits & légumes
La pensée et le mouvant
Ich und du und so weiter

11 **7 Fragen an das Leben**
Was? Wäre? Wenn?
Wer ist der Grösste?
Wo kommt das her?
Qui dominera le monde ?
Warum wackeln Wolkenkratzer?
I used to know that

12 **Taste and other tales**
Saveurs d'hier & d'aujourd'hui
Das Parfum
Die Rose
Dolce Jasmine
Peau de pêche
Bitterschokolade
Ich bin so wild nach Kirschsorbet
Ich bin so wild nach deinem Erdbeermund
Hello my big big honey!
Souviens-toi
Le jardin des amoureux

13 **Unberechenbar**
Fiquei com o seu número
Les mille et une nuits
Tausendschön
111 lieux à Bienne
Hundert Jahre Freiheit
99 francs
Fifty fifty
Eine Frau von fünfzig Jahren
Quarantine
Vingt défis pour la planète...
13 à table
Die zwölf wilden Schwäne
La onzième souris verte
Dix petites anarchistes
Neuf parfaits étrangers
Acht Berge
Sieben Tage, sieben Nächte
Sechs Personen suchen einen Autor
Cinq galops de chevaux
Four quartets
Drei Schritte
Deux chats sous un même toit
Eindeutig zweideutig
Einmal ist keinmal
Zeros + ones
Moins que zéro
Di impossibile non c'è niente

14 **Cher inconnu**
Wo bist du zu Hause?
Das geträumte Land
Niemandsland
Borderline
Sans domicile fixe
Clandestino
Dein Name geht dir voraus
Dies ist kein Reiseführer

15 **Klima**
Collapse
De Wind hed gcheert
Radikale Veränderungen stehen bevor
100 Dinge, die man diesen Sommer gemacht haben sollte
Un été pas comme les autres
The last summer
Mamma mia! Was haben wir geweint
Le déluge
Steig oder stirb
Was tun, wenn's brennt?
Bir Şey Yap! Tut was!
Man tut was man kann
Die Welt ist verkehrt, nicht wir!
Wie wollen wir leben?
Wann wird es endlich wieder so
Wie es nie war
Wir haben noch viel vor
Keine Ahnung, ob das richtig ist
Weisst du, dass die Bäume reden
The grass is singing
Le chant des abeilles
À l'écoute
... und ich höre doch!
Die Erde liebt uns
Ich habe sie geliebt
Die letzten ihrer Art
Terra, ar, fogo e água
Jamaiplus
J'ai tout essayé !
Honte à vous !

16 **Un jour tu verras...**
Was ich euch nicht erzählte
How to write
How to fail
Wie wird Beton zu Gras
Wie sie ein Schreiben schrieben
Wie ein Blatt im Herbstwind
Wie man es vermasselt
Comment chier dans les bois
Comment devenir maître du monde
Wie man sich die Welt erlebt
Wie die Lilien auf dem Felde
... wie der Hauch eines Büffels im Winter
Wie alles funktioniert
Das hätt' ich vorher wissen müssen

17 **Last Lecture**
Das letzte Wort
Am Ende der Strasse
Am Ende ich
Am Hang
Am Ende ein Anfang
Irgendwas ist immer

How books make books
On a poetry of the everyday by Sadie Plant

> "If only you knew from what rubbish
> Poetry grows, knowing no shame"
>
> Anna Akhmatova, *Secrets of the Craft*, 21 January 1940

Comment lire a bookshelf in einem Buch was first installed as *Comment lire a bookshelf in zwei Teilen* in an empty former telephone box on a platform in the station at Biel/Bienne, where trains between Zurich and Geneva cross every day. The train line is itself a link between the German and French-speaking parts of Switzerland, not to mention Italian, English, Albanian, Arabic, Portuguese and the many other languages which meet in Switzerland and, especially, in Biel/Bienne.

During the exhibition period, people who used the platform every day could look into the illuminated booth, in which books were not stacked vertically but horizontally on shelves. A few were scattered on the floor, as if someone had thrown them off the shelves. The booth was locked, there was no signage. Only two QR codes stuck onto the glass led to the digital trail of poems that could be downloaded and read on a smartphone. The artist was not mentioned. Emilie Guenat and Florence Jung, who curated the exhibition, also remained undercover in the secret place.

Sadie Plant had arranged a wide variety of found titles into several piles, each a poem composed from the writing on their spines. Some took up several shelves and at first glance appeared to be uneven and disordered, since it was the titles themselves that were aligned. The pool from which she drew her lyrical lines was largely composed of books found on public bookshelves, to be given and taken away for free, most of them more usually thought of, even belittled, as shallow entertainment literature—romance novels, self-help books, travel guides and recipes, pulp fiction.

Some she found she could not use, perhaps because of typography that was difficult to read or designs that gave too much space to the name of book's author, or because their colours and sizes simply didn't fit. A few books had to be bought to make the poems work. Some pay homage to local authors or the work of friends; one of her own books, *Zeros and Ones*, even appears in "Unberechenbar" [13].

One of the influences on Sadie Plant's work is that of Natalie Czech, whose artist book *Je n'ai rien à dire. Seulement à montrer. / Ich habe nichts zu sagen. Nur zu zeigen. / I have nothing to say. Only to show,* was published by our house in 2012. Natalie Czech placed the title in a speech bubble on the bright yellow cover of a work which in turn recalls Walter Benjamin's *Arcades*, the project in which he assembled his nineteenth century philosophy of history from the perspective of the twentieth century as a vast collection of quotations, excerpts, and notes. The work was published posthumously in 1982 and is considered one of the most important fragments of German literature and, among other things, a precursor of postmodernism because it anticipated the methods of Appropriation Art of the 1970s and 80s.

Appropriation is a key word here: Natalie Czech marked individual letters and words in found texts—newspaper articles, exhibition texts, letters—which were then combined to form poems that someone else had already written. "A hidden poem by Rolf Dieter Brinkmann", for example, can be found in a text about the American conceptual artist Louise Lawler, who showed her first solo exhibition at the Metro Pictures gallery in New York in 1982. Louise Lawler, known for her institutional critique, and the German beatnik poet Rolf Dieter Brinkmann (1940–1975) make a joint appearance in this text, in which the letters are highlighted with a purple marker:

> Surprising
> the random arrangement
> of the ashtray
> the cup, the
> hand to form a closed picture.
> It cannot be said
> that anything lives here.

Rolf Dieter Brinkmann's poem seems to have been inserted into the exhibition text about Louise Lawler as if by chance. The lyrical lines emerge from the fabric of the text, language and image enter into a dialogue. Natalie Czech said about her series *Hidden Poems*, which is part of her book *Je n'ai rien à dire. Seulement à montrer. / I have nothing to say. Only to show. / I have nothing to say. Only to show* is: "The poems find their text. And the texts find their poems."

Unlike Natalie Czech, Sadie Plant uses the book titles as bases on which new poems can emerge. She does not amend the lettering or highlight certain words, but rather allows her material to speak for itself.

The relationship is one of mutuality: poems find their books, and books their poems too.

Sadie Plant's book not only ties in with publications in our programme in terms of content and form, but also translates an installation into a book. *Comment lire a bookshelf in einem Buch* pursues our own engagement with books not only as containers for content, but also as objects of long duration, material features of the book landscape. This work consists of titles that have already been discarded or thrown away, fed into the cycle of re-reading and re-use. This is a form of poetic sustainability that fits perfectly with our concept of bookmaking. All books are made from other books, even from those left on the shelf.

Anne König

7 Fragen an das Leben, Dirk von Nayhauss, Edition Braus im Wachter Verlag, Heidelberg, 2005
→ 11

13 à table *! 2021*, Tonino Benacquista et al., Pocket, Paris, 2020
→ 13

99 francs*. (14,99 €)*, Frédéric Beigbeder, Éditions Grasset et Fasquelle, Paris, 2000
→ 13

100 Dinge die man diesen Sommer gemacht haben sollte, Migros-Genossenschafts-Bund, Zürich, 2014
→ 15

100 Shades of White, Preethi Nair, Harper Collins, London, 2004
→ 2

111 lieux à Bienne *à ne pas manquer*, Sonja Muhlert, Emons Verlag, Cologne, 2020
→ 13

Acht Berge, Paolo Cognetti, Penguin Verlag, München, 2016
→ 13

Ach, wär ich nur zu Hause geblieben*. Lustige Geschichten rund ums Verreisen*, Kerstin Gier, Bastei Lübbe Taschenbücher, Bergisch Gladbach, 2007
→ 7

A Day's Work*. Selected by Susan Morris*, Stiftung Konzeptuelle Kunst Soest, Soest, 2019
→ 6

Afin que naisse le jour, Anne LeClaire, Édition France Loisirs, Paris, 2002
→ 6

À l'écoute *de vos sens*, Nicky Kinnard, Éditions Gründ, Paris, 2003
→ 15

Am Ende der Strasse, Dylan Wickrama und Martina Zürcher, Zürcher Publishing, Aarberg, 2016
→ 17

Am Ende ein Anfang, Barbara Bronnen, Arche Literatur Verlag, Zürich und Hamburg, 2006
→ 17

Am Ende ich, Ariane Grundies, Kein & Aber, Zürich, 2006
→ 17

Am Hang, Markus Werner, Fischer Taschenbuch Verlag, Frankfurt am Main, 2009
→ 17

Are You My Mother?, P.D. Eastman, Random House, New York, 1962
→ 5

Aufbruch in ein unbekanntes Land. *Von Ägypten nach Kanaan*, John Drane, Brunnen Verlag, Giessen 1995
→ 7

Au fil du temps. *Activités créatrices sur textiles*, Commission romande des moyens d'enseignement (COROME), Neuchâtel, 1988
→ 6

Auf verbotenen Wegen. *Die Rückkehr einer Iranerin in ihre Heimat*, Hélène Kafi, Knaur Taschenbuch, München, 1993
→ 7

Avant de te dire adieu, Mary Higgins Clark, Éditions Albin Michel, Paris, 2000
→ 1

A Year from Monday. *New lectures and writings by John Cage*, Wesleyan University Press, Hanover, 1969
→ 6

Beautiful Secrets. Das Spiel beginnt, Lisi Harrison, Arena Verlag, Würzburg, 2013
→ 3

Bir Şey Yap! *Aktif demokrasi için çagri.* **Tut was!** *Pläydoyer für eine aktive Demokratie*, Can Dündar, Hoffmann and Campe Verlag, Hamburg, 2018
→ 15

Bitterschokolade, Mirjam Pressler, Belz & Gelberg, Weinheim und Basel, 2006
→ 12

Borderline. *À un compagnon disparu*, Anne-Catherine Menétrey-Savary, Éditions d'en bas, Lausanne, 2009
→ 14

Carnaval noir, Metin Arditi, Éditions Grasset & Fasquelle, Paris, 2018
→ 2

Cher inconnu, Berlie Doherty, Éditions Gallimard Jeunesse, Paris, 2002
→ 14

Cinq galops de chevaux, René Guillot, Odège, Paris, 1967
→ 13

Clandestino. *Un reportage d'Hubert Paris – Envoyé spécial*, Éditions Glénat, Grenoble, 2014
→ 14

Collapse. *Philosophical Research and Development, Vol. IV*, Robin Mackay ed., Urbanomic, Falmouth, 2010
→ 15

Colours of Love. *Verführt*, Kathryn Taylor, Weltbild, Augsburg, 2017
→ 2

Comme le fleuve qui coule. *Récits 1998-2005*, Paulo Coelho, Éditions France Loisirs, Paris, 2006
→ 6

Comment chier dans les bois. *Pour une approche environnementale d'un art perdu,* Kathleen Meyer, Edimontagne, Servoz, 2001
→ 16

Comment devenir maître du monde *en vingt-six leçons et demie*, Dan Gutman, Bayard Éditions Jeunesse, Paris, 2004
→ 16

Das dreifarbene Meer. *Meine Heilsgeschichte – eine Bibliographie*, Silja Walter, Paulus-Verlag, Freiburg, 2009
→ 2

Das geträumte Land, Imbolo Mbue, Verlag Kiepenheuer & Witsch, Köln, 2017
→ 14

Das hätt' ich vorher wissen müssen, Evelyn Sanders, Wilhelm Heyne Verlag, München, 2000
→ 16

Das kann ich selbst! *501 Tipps und Kniffe für Geräte, die nicht mehr funktionieren wollen*, Reader's Digest Deutschland, Stuttgart, 2014
→ 4

Das letzte Wort, Hanif Kureishi, S. Fischer Verlag, Frankfurt am Main, 2015
→ 17

Das Parfum. *Die Geschichte eines Mörders,* Patrick Süskind, Diogenes Verlag, Zürich, 1994
→ 12

Das wissen wir schon, Noemi Schneider, Carl Hanser Verlag, München, 2017
→ 5

Dein Name geht dir voraus, Maria Nurowska, dtv, München, 2007
→ 14

Denken und Sprechen, L.S. Wygotski, Fischer Taschenbuch Verlag, Frankfurt, 1979
→ 10

Der blaue See ist heute grün, Jutta Treiber, Esslingen Édition J&V, Esslingen, 1996
→ 2

Der Teil und das Ganze. *Gespräche im Umkreis der Atomphysik*, Werner Heisenberg, Piper Verlag, München, 2017
→ 10

Der Wolf und die sieben jungen Geisslein, Brüder Grimm, SBS-Märchenbuch, Zürich, 2022
→ 10

***Deux chats sous un même toit**. Scènes de la vie quotidienne*, Patti Davis & Ward Schumaker, Hors Collection, Paris, 2007
→ 13

De Wind hed gcheert, Max Huwyler, Zytglogge Verlag, Bern, 1993
→ 15

***Die Erde liebt uns**. Sprüche und Gesänge indianischer Naturerfahrung*, Meinrad Faltner, Edition Christian Brandstätter, Wien, 1984
→ 15

***Die Farbe von Glück**. Ein Roman über das Ankommen*, Clara Maria Bagus, Piper Verlag, München, 2020
→ 2

Die fröhliche Moritat von der Bleibe, Michel Layaz, verlag die brotsuppe, Biel/Bienne, 2014
→ 7

Die goldenen Schlüssel, Hans Köningsberger, Walter-Verlag, Olten und Freiburg im Breisgau, 1980
→ 2

***Die kleinen Dinge machen das Leben schön**. Was wir von den Alten lernen können*, Karl Pillemer, Piper Verlag, München, 2014
→ 9

Die kleinsten, stillsten Dinge, Sara Baume, Rohwohlt Verlag, Reinbek bei Hamburg, 2016
→ 9

***Die Letzten ihrer Art**. Eine Reise zu den aussterbenden Tieren unserer Erde*, Douglas Adams & Mark Carwardine, Wilhelm Heyne Verlag, München, 2007
→ 15

***Die Pilger und die Reisenden**. Roman aus Sydney*, Alice Ekert-Rotholz, Rowohlt Taschenbuch Verlag, Reinbek bei Hamburg, 1970
→ 7

***Die Reise nach Hause**. Die Geschichte von Michael Thomas und den sieben Engelwesen*, Lee Carroll, KOHA-Verlag, Dorfen, 2014
→ 7

Die Rose, Robert Walser, Suhrkamp Verlag, Zürich und Frankfurt am Main, 2015
→ 12

Dies ist kein Reiseführer, Nikki Busch, Carlsen Verlag, Hamburg, 2013
→ 14

***Die Welt ist verkehrt, nicht wir!** Katharina von Arx und Freddy Drilhon*, Wilfried Meichtry, Nagel & Kimche, München, 2015
→ 15

Die Zeit danach, Cordula Broicher, Qindie, 2014
→ 7

Die zwölf wilden Schwäme. *Eine Reise ins Reich der Magie*, Starhawk & Hilary Valentine, Verlag Hermann Bauer, Freiburg im Breisgau, 2001
→ 13

Di impossibile non c'è niente, Andrea Vitali, Adriano Salani Editore, Milano, 2014
→ 13

Dirty Pretty Things, Michael Faudet, Self-published, 2014
→ 9

Dix petites anarchistes, Daniel de Roulet, Éditions Buchet/Chastel, Paris, 2018
→ 13

Dolce Jasmine, Bertrice Small, Mondolibri, Milano, 1999
→ 12

Drei Schritte. *Interkantonales Lesebuch für das dritte Schuljahr. Band 2*, Lehrmittelverlag des Kantons Zürich, 1984
→ 13

Dr Jekyll and Mr Hyde, Robert Louis Stevenson, Oxford Bookworms Library, Oxford, 2008
→ 10

Dumm gelaufen. *600 Missgeschicke mit Todesfolge*, Cynthia Ceilán, Bastei Lübbe, Köln, 2011
→ 8

Eindeutig zweideutig, Reinhard Habeck, Tosa Verlag, Wien, 2004
→ 13

Eine Frau von fünfzig Jahren, William Somerset Maugham, dvt, München, 1991
→ 13

Eine Geschichte, die uns verbindet, Guillaume Musso, Pendo Verlag, München, 2021
→ 1

Einfach für zwei. *92 Rezepte saisonal, abwechslungsreich, natürlich mit Schweizer Milchprodukten*, Zentralverband schweizerischer Milchproduzenten (ZVSM), Bern, 1998
→ 6

Einmal ist keinmal, Janet Evanovich, Wilhelm Goldmann Verlag, München, 1997
→ 13

Endstation Venedig. *Commissario Brunettis zweiter Fall*, Donna Leon, Diogenes Verlag, Zürich, 1995
→ 7

Fifty Fifty, Steve Cavanagh, Orion Publishing, London, 2020
→ 13

Fiquei com o seu número, Sophie Kinsella, Editora Record, Rio de Janeiro, 2012
→ 13

Flug mit Elisabeth, Walter Ackermann, Benziger Jugendtaschenbücher, Zürich, 1957
→ 7

Four Quartets, T.S. Eliot, Faber and Faber, London, 1958
→ 13

Fruits & légumes, Anthony Palou, Édition France Loisirs, Paris, 2011
→ 10

Gebt uns eine Chance! *Ein engagierter Bericht über die Arbeit mit Jugendlichen im Abseits*, John B. Simon, Kösel-Verlag, München, 1984
→ 4

'Hello my Big Big Honey!'. *Love Letters to Bangkok Bar Girls and Their Revealing Interviews*, Dave Walker and Richard S. Ehrlich, Dragon Dance Publications, Bangkok, 1998
→ 12

Hidden in Plain Sight. *How to find and execute your company's next big growth strategy*, Erich Joachimsthaler, Havard Business School Press, Boston, 2007
→ 3

Hinter dem Bahnhof, Arno Carmenisch, Engeler Verlag, Schupfart, 2019
→ 7

Honte à vous ! *Par les signataires de la pétition pour sauver la Demeure du Chaos*, Édition Musée de l'organe, Saint-Romain-au-Mont d'Or, 2008
→ 15

How to Fail. *Warum wir erst durch Scheitern richtig stark werden*, Wilhelm Goldmann Verlag, München, 2020
→ 16

How to Write, Gertrude Stein, Dover Publications, New York, 1975
→ 16

Hundert Jahre Freiheit *ohne Gleichberechtigung*, James Baldwin, Rowohlt Taschenbuch Verlag, Reinbek bei Hamburg, 1964
→ 13

Ich bin so wild nach deinem Erdbeermund, Klaus Kinski, Wilhelm Heyne Verlag, München, 1979
→ 12

Ich bin so wild nach Kirschsorbet. *Coole Frauen und heisse Rezepte*, Mary Jane Ryan, dtv, München, 1998
→ 12

Ich dich auch*. Ein Episodenroman für Paarungsgestörte*, Güzin Kar, Kein & Aber, Zürich, 2006
→ 1

Ich habe sie geliebt, Anna Gavalda, Fischer Taschenbuch Verlag, Frankfurt am Main, 2004
→ 15

Ich treffe dich zwischen den Zeilen, Stephanie Butland, Knaur Taschenbuch, München, 2017
→ 3

Ich und du und so weiter*. Kleine Einführung in die Sozialpsychologie*, Otto Marmet, Beltz Taschenbuch, Weinheim und Basel, 1996
→ 10

Ich will verstehen, was du wirklich brauchst*. Gewaltfreie Kommunikation mit Kindern. Das Projekt Giraffentraum*, Frank & Gundi Gaschler, Kösel-Verlag, München, 2007
→ 1

Il colore trasparente della notte, Pam Jenoff, Edizione Mondadori Direct, Milano, 2013
→ 2

Abgefahren! ***Im Zug mit Katja Walder****. Pendelgeschichten*, Katja Walder, Limmat Verlag, Zürich, 2012
→ 7

Indigo *or, Mapping the Waters*, Marina Warner, Vintage Books, London, 1993
→ 2

Irgendwas ist immer, Tine Wittler, S. Fischer Verlag, Frankfurt am Main, 2007
→ 17

I Used to Know That*. Geography stuff you forgot from school*, Will Williams, Michael O'Mara Books, London, 2010
→ 11

'J'ai tout essayé !'*. Opposition, pleurs et crises de rage : traverser sans dommage la période de 1 à 5 ans*, Isabelle Filliozat et Anouk Dubois, Éditions Jean-Claude Lattès, Paris, 2011
→ 15

Jamaiplu, Josiane Balasko, Pygmalion, Paris, 2019
→ 15

Jusqu'à l'impensable, Michael Connelly, Éditions Calmann-Levy, Paris, 2017
→ 7

Jusqu'au bout de l'amour, Heinz G. Konsalik, Presses Pocket, Paris, 1981
→ 7

Jusqu'au bout de la terre*. Parcours d'un géographe*, Claude Collin Delavaud, Éditions Arthaud, Paris, 2005
→ 7

Keine Ahnung, ob das richtig ist, Julia Engelmann, Wilhelm Goldmann Verlag, München, 2019
→ 15

Klima. *Die Kraft mit dem wir leben*, Pro Futura Verlag, München, 1994
→ 15

Komm, ich erzähl dir eine Geschichte, Jorge Bucay, Ammann Verlag, Zürich, 2005
→ 1

La carte et le territoire, Michel Houellebecq, Flammarion, Paris, 2010
→ 10

La cordée de l'espoir, Maurice Metral, Éditions de la Matze, Sion, 1974
→ 6

Laisse-moi te raconter... les chemins de la vie, Jorge Bucay, Oh ! Éditions, Paris, 2004
→ 1

Lange Weile. *Über das Warten*, Andrea Köhler, Insel Verlag, Frankfurt am Main, 2007
→ 6

La onzième souris verte, Christian Poslaniec, L'école des loisirs, Paris, 2007
→ 13

La pensée et le mouvant, Henri Bergson, Quadrige/Presses Universitaires de France (PUF), Paris, 1987
→ 10

La souris verte, Robert Sabatier, Édition du Club France Loisirs, Paris, 1990
→ 2

Lass endlich los und lebe. Lebe was Dich glücklich macht, Richard J. Leider & David A. Shapiro, Weltbild, München, 2006
→ 4

Lass mich, doch verlass mich nicht. *ADHS und Partnerschaft*, Cordula Neuhaus, dtv, München, 2017
→ 1

Last Lecture. *Die Lehren meines Lebens*, Randy Pausch mit Jeffrey Zaslow, Wilhelm Goldmann Verlag, München, 2010
→ 17

La tante Julia et le scribouillard, Mario Vargas Llosa, Éditions Gallimard, Paris, 1979
→ 10

Laufen. *Alles über Ausrüstung, Technik, Training, Ernährung und Laufmedizin*, Dr. Thomas Wessinghage, BLV, München, 2004
→ 8

La verità non ha colore. *Aguzzini e vittime dell'apartheid testimoniano alla Commissione per la verità e la riconciliazione sudafricana*, Danilo Franchi & Laura Miani, Edizioni Comedit 2000, Milano, 2003
→ 2

La vie en roux, François Vorpe, Éditions du ROC, Saint-Imier, 2019
→ 2

Le barbare et les jonquilles. *Les enquêtes de l'inspecteur Perrin*, Michel Bory, Éditions de l'Aire, Vevey, 1995
→ 10

Le chant des abeilles. *Restaurer notre alliance avec l'abondance*, Jacqueline Freeman, Mama Éditions, Paris, 2017
→ 15

Le Déluge. *Un roman à l'usage des dépravés tant du point de vue moral que technique*, Jon Ferguson, Castagniééé, Vevey, 2010
→ 15

Le Diable et le bon Dieu, Jean-Paul Sartre, Éditions Gallimard, Paris, 1951
→ 10

Le hasard et la nécessité. *Essai sur la philosophie naturelle de la biologie moderne*, Jacques Monod, Éditions du Seuil, Paris, 1970
→ 10

Le jardin des amoureux. *Les 50 noms de l'amour d'Ibn Qayyim al-Jawziyya*, Fatema Mernissi, Éditions Marsam, Rabat, 2011
→ 12

Le librerie e lo studio. *n. 11*, Aberto Peruzzo Editore, Milano, 1974
→ 10

Le noir est une couleur, Grisélidis Réal, Éditions Balland, Paris, 1974
→ 2

Les mille et une nuits, Sindbad Le Marin, Éditions J'ai Lu, Paris, 2019
→ 13

Light Years, James Salter, Vintage Books, New York, 1995
→ 6

Links und rechts vom Glück, Silke Schütze, Knaur Taschenbuch Verlag, München, 2011
→ 3

Lire une image. *Analyse de contenu iconique*, Marie-Claude Vettraino-Soulard, Armand Colin Éditeur, Paris, 1993
→ 4

Mach's bunt. *Inspiration zur Innendekoration vom schwedischen Farbexperten Per Nimér*, Lannoo Publisher, Tielt, 2005
→ 2

Mamma mia! Was haben wir geweint, Gardi Hutter und Catherine Louis, Nord-Süd Verlag, Zürich, 1999
→ 15

Man tut, was man kann, Hans Rath, Wunderlich Verlag, Reinbek bei Hamburg, 2009
→ 15

Moins que zéro, Bret Easton Ellis, Éditions 10/18, Paris, 1985
→ 13

Henry Moore: ***Mother and Child***, Mentor-Unesco Art Books, New York, 1966
→ 10

Murder on the Orient Express, Agatha Christie, Fontana/Collins, Glasgow, 1979
→ 7

Nachtzug nach Lissabon, Pascal Mercier, btb Verlag, München, 2006
→ 7

Neon Pink & Blue, X Schneeberger, verlag die brotsuppe, Biel/Bienne, 2020
→ 2

Neuf parfaits étrangers, Liane Moriarty, Éditions Albin Michel, Paris, 2020
→ 13

Niemandsland, Utta Danella, Pavillon Verlag, München, 2006
→ 14

Nordwärts. *Eine Frau mit 30 Huskys in der Wildnis*, Silvia Furtwängler, Rowohlt Taschenbuch Verlag, Reinbek bei Hamburg, 2015
→ 7

Ohne Schnur. *Kunst und Drahtlose Kommunikation*, Katja Kwastek, Revolver, Frankfurt am Main, 2004
→ 6

Ogni parola è un seme, Susanna Tamaro, Rizzoli, Milano, 2005
→ 9

One Way or Another. *Zwei Wege zu dir*, Kara McDowell, Loewe Verlag, Bindlach, 2021
→ 5

Où es-tu ?, Marc Levy, Éditions Robert Laffont, Paris, 2009
→ 7

Papa, was ist ein Fremder? *Gespräch mit meiner Tochter*, Tahar Ben Jelloun, Rowohlt Verlag, Berlin, 1999
→ 5

Peau de pêche, Jodi Lynn Anderson, Éditions Albin Michel, Paris, 2006
→ 12

Pour un jour avec toi, Gayle Forman, Pocket, Paris, 2013
→ 7

Quarantine, Jim Crace, Penguin Books, London, 1998
→ 13

Qui dominera le Monde ?, Pierre Lanarès, Éditions S.D.T., Dammarie-les-Lys, 1957
→ 11

Radikale Veränderungen stehen bevor. *Wohin führen Sie?*, Dr. Hans Heinz, Advent-Verlag, Zürich, 1993
→ 15

Regardez-moi, *Gudule*, Flammarion Jeunesse, Paris, 2001
→ 1

Reise nach Jerusalem, Margit Pfüger, Verlag der Francke-Buchhandlung, Marburg an der Lahn, 2003
→ 7

Reise nach Ostpreussen, Westpreussen und Danzig. *Wiedersehen mit der Heimat heute*, Wilhelm Matull, Gräfe und Unzer Verlag, München, 1975
→ 7

Retour d'Afrique, Corinne Hofmann, Presses du Belvédère, Sainte-Croix, 2007
→ 7

Rotes Meer, Åke Edwardson, List Taschenbuch, Berlin, 2009
→ 2

Rücken an Rücken, Julia Franck, Fischer Taschenbuch Verlag, Frankfurt am Main, 2013
→ 3

Rumeurs, Anna Godbersen, Éditions Albin Michel, Paris, 2009
→ 9

Sag es mit Versen. *850 Glückwunsch-Verse und andere Reime zu allen passenden und unpassenden Gelegenheiten und Verlegenheiten. Eine Reimkunde mit ausführlichen Anleitungen zum Selbermachen*, Friedrich Morgenroth, Panorama Verlag, Wiesbaden
→ 4

Sammeln und Sichten. *Ein kritischer Rückblick nach einem Vierteljahrhundert erfolgreichen Wirkens im Dienst kranker, leidender Mitmenschen*, P. Thomas Häberle, Veritas Verlag, Linz, 1985
→ 10

Sans domicile fixe, Edouard Michel, auto-édition, Saint-Magne de Castillon, 1993
→ 14

Sans retour, Patricia Macdonald, Éditions Albin Michel, Paris, 1990
→ 7

Saveurs d'hier & d'aujourd'hui, classeur, IMP Sàrl/IMP BV
→ 12

Sechs Personen suchen einen Autor, Luigi Pirandello, Philipp Reclam jun. Verlag, Stuttgart, 1991
→ 13

Selfies. *Der siebte Fall für Carl Mørck, Sonderdezernat Q*, Jussi Adler-Olsen, dtv, München, 2017
→ 9

Sieben Tage, sieben Nächte, Karen Gillece, Club Premiere, München, 2005
→ 13

Sieh mich an, Mareike Krügel, Piper Verlag, München, 2017
→ 1

Sind Sie meine Tochter? *Leben mit meiner alzheimerkranken Mutter*, Gabriela Zander-Schneider, Weltbild, Augsburg, 2011
→ 5

So rot wie Blut, Salla Simukka, Arena Verlag, Würzburg, 2014
→ 2

Souviens-toi, Mary Higgins Clark, Édition France Loisirs, Paris, 1994
→ 12

So weiss wie Schnee, Salla Simukka, Arena Verlag, Würzburg, 2015
→ 2

Sprung auf die Plattform. *Junge Schweizer Literatur*, Verlag Nagel & Kimche, Zürich, 1998
→ 7

Steig oder stirb. *Geständnisse eines Bergsüchtigen*, Mark Twight, Piper Verlag, München, 2007
→ 15

Stolz und Vorurteil, Jane Austen, dtv, München, 1997
→ 10

Storia di chi fugge e di chi resta. *L'amica geniale, Volume Terzo*, Elena Ferrante, Edizioni e/o, Roma, 2020
→ 7

Sucre brun, Nancy Cato, Éditions Belfond, Paris, 1993
→ 2

Süss und Sauer. *Kolumnen aus Asien*, Peter Achten, Friedrich Reinhardt Verlag, Basel, 2008
→ 10

Tais-toi et plonge!, Claudine Mouly, Éditions Calmann-Lévy, Paris, 1982
→ 4

Taste and Other Tales, Roald Dahl, Addison Wesley Longman, Harlow, 1997
→ 12

Tausendschön, Kristina Ohlsson, Blanvalet Verlag, München, 2013
→ 13

Terra, Ar, Fogo e Aqua. *O poder transformador da energia*, Scott Cunningham, Editorial Estampa, Lisboa, 2000
→ 15

Texte, Daten, Bilder, Franz Hohler, Luchterhand Literaturverlag, Hamburg und Zürich, 1993
→ 9

The Colour of Law, Mark Gimenez, Sphere, London, 2009
→ 2

The Grass is Singing, Doris Lessing, Flamingo Modern Classics, London, 1994
→ 15

The Last Summer, Boris Pasternak, Penguin Books, London, 1960
→ 15

Törtchen & Kleingebäck. *Verführerisch süss & himmlisch gut*, Planet Medien, Köln
→ 10

Transsibérien. *Un voyage mythique en train*, Lonely Planet Publications, Paris, 2002
→ 7

Tu es. Tu es nicht., S.J. Watson, Fisher Taschenbuch Verlag, Frankfurt am Main, 2016
→ 1

Unberechenbar. *Das Leben ist mehr als eine Gleichung*, Harald Lesch und Thomas Schwartz, Verlag Herder, Freiburg im Breisgau, 2020
→ 13

... und fahr'n wir ohne Wiederkehr. *Von Ostpreussen nach Sibirien 1944–1949*, Fritz Blankenhorn, Rohwolt Taschenbuch Verlag, Reinbek bei Hamburg, 2006
→ 7

... und ich höre doch! *Ein technologisches Abenteuer zwischen Silicon Valley und den Alpen*, Geoffrey Ball, Haymon Verlag, Innsbruck, 2011
→ 15

Un été pas comme les autres, Heinz G. Konsalik, Presses de la Cité, Paris, 1977
→ 15

Un fleuve, un amour, Luis Cernuda, Éditions Fata Morgana, Saint-Clément-de-Rivière, 1985
→ 9

Un grand week-end *à Venise*, Hachette Tourisme, Paris, 2013
→ 7

Un jour tu verras..., Mary Higgins Clark, Éditions Albin Michel, Paris, 1993
→ 16

Unterwegs, Mark Twain, Verlag Werner Dausien, Hanau, 1988
→ 7

Meine Welt der Fahrzeuge. ***Unterwegs mit dem Zug***, Ravensburger Buchverlag, Ravensburg, 2017
→ 7

Un week-end fou, Gary Soto, Castor Poche Flammarion, Paris, 1996
→ 7

Vent dessus, vent dedans, Marin-Marie, Éditions Gallimard, Paris, 2000
→ 4

Vingt défis pour la planète, *vingt ans pour y faire face*, Jean-François Rischard, Actes Sud, Arles, 2003
→ 13

Vivre avec les couleurs, Janine Mora, Éditions Recto-Verseau, Romont, 1993
→ 2

Voices. *Seychelles short stories*, Glynn Burridge, Nighthue Publications, Seychelles, 2000
→ 9

Voyages sans frontières, Pierre Daninos, Sélection du Reader's Digest, Paris, 1970
→ 7

Wann wird es endlich wieder so, wie es nie war. *Alle Toten fliegen hoch. Teil 2*, Joachim Meyerhoff, Verlag Kiepenheuer & Witsch, Köln, 2020
→ 15

Warum wackeln Wolkenkratzer? *111 verblüffende Fragen und Antworten zur Technik*, Norbert Landa, Arena Verlag, Würzburg, 1993
→ 11

Was ich euch nicht erzählte, Celeste Ng, dtv, München, 2020
→ 16

Was tun, wenn's brennt?, Ulrich Hoffmann, Knaur Taschenbuch, München, 2002
→ 15

Was? Wäre? Wenn?, Wiebke Lorenz, Piper Verlag, München, Zürich, 2003
→ 11

Was zeigt die Uhr? *Mit den verstellbaren Zeigern learnst Du die Uhrzeit im Nu*, Parragon Books, Bath, 2008
→ 6

*Mitakuye Oyasin: '**We Are All Related**'*, Dr. A.C. Ross, Bear Publications, Ft. Yates, 1990
→ 5

Weisst du, dass die Bäume reden. *Weisheit der Indianer*, Herder & Co, Freiburg im Breisgau, 1992
→ 15

Wer ist der Grösste?, Paul Maar & Peter Gut, Verlag Friedrich Oetinger, Hamburg, 2004
→ 11

Westwärts mit der Nacht, Beryl Markham, Weltbild, München, 1987
→ 7

Why Contribute to the Spread of Ugliness?, Stuart Whipps, Ikon Gallery, Birmingham, 2012
→ 9

Wie alles funktioniert, Michael Wright und Mukul Patel, Mondo Verlag, Vevey, 2001
→ 16

... wie der Hauch eines Büffels im Winter. *Indianische Selbstzeugnisse*, T.C. McLuhan, Hoffmann und Campe Verlag, Hamburg, 1979
→ 16

Wie die Lilien auf dem Felde. *Auf Gott vertrauen*, Gisbert von Spankeren, Verlag am Bimbach, Bimbach, 1995
→ 16

Wie ein Blatt im Herbstwind, Janette Oke, Verlag Klaus Gerth, Asslar, 1991
→ 16

Wie man es vermasselt, George Watsky, Diogenes Verlag, Zürich, 2017
→ 16

Wie man sich die Welt erlebt. *Das ~~Kunst~~Alltagsmuseeum zum mitnehmen*, Keri Smith, Verlag Antje Kunstmann, München, 2011
→ 16

Von Hündchen und Kätzchen. ***Wie sie ein Schreiben schrieben***, Josef Čapek, Nakladatelstvi Milos Uhlir-Baset, Praha, 2004
→ 16

Wie wird Beton zu Gras. *Fast eine Liebesgeschichte*, Otto F. Walter, Rowohlt Taschenbuch Verlag, Reinbek bei Hamburg, 1992
→ 16

Wie wollen wir leben?, Peter Bieri, dtv, München, 2011
→ 15

Wir haben noch viel vor. *Frauen um die Fünfzig*, Regine Schneider, Fischer Taschenbuch Verlag, Frankfurt am Main, 2000
→ 15

Wir in 3 Worten, Mhairi McFarlane, Knaur Taschenbuch, München 2013
→ 9

Wo bist du zu Hause?, Marion Goedelt, Thienemann-Esslinger Verlag, Stuttgart, 2021
→ 14

Wohin die Liebe dich auch führt, Sara MacDonald, Bastei Lübbe Taschenbücher, Bergisch Gladbach, 2007
→ 7

Wo kommt das her? *Vom Rohstoff zu T-Shirt, Apfelsaft und Co.*, Karolin Küntzel und Kathleen Richter, Compact Verlag, München, 2015
→ 11

Wo warst du, Robert?, Hans Magnus Enzensberger, Carl Hanser Verlag, München und Wien, 1998
→ 7

Yo, Brothers and Sisters. *Siamo o non siamo un bel movimento?*, Jovanotti, Fratelli Vallardi Editori, Milano, 1988
→ 5

Zeros + Ones. *Digital Women + the New Technoculture*, Sadie Plant, Fourth Estate, London, 1997
→ 13

Zurück, Fabian Vogt, Gerth Medien, Asslar, 2002
→ 7

This book was published following the exhibition of Sadie Plant, *Comment lire a bookshelf in zwei Teilen*, from October 2021 to January 2022, at the secret place in Biel/Bienne.

Edited by
the secret place

Copyediting and Proofreading
Emilie Guenat, Anne König, Sadie Plant

Design
Nicolas Eigenheer

Typeface
Executive (www.optimo.ch)

Lithography
Courvoisier-Gassmann SA, Biel/Bienne

Printing and binding
Musumeci S.p.A, Quart

Acknowledgments
Coline Houot, Florence Jung, Nicolas Leuba, Lars Meyer, Bea Schlingelhoff, Louis Schneeberger, Sebastian Verdon

This book was supported by

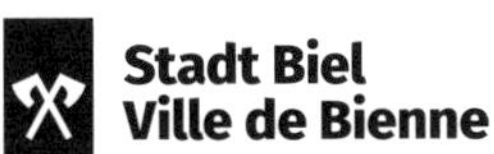

SWISSLOS
Culture Canton de Berne

Fondation
Jan Michalski

Published by
Spector Books
Verlagsgesellschaft mbH
Harkortstraße 10
04107 Leipzig
www.spectorbooks.com

Distribution
GE, AT: GVA, Gemeinsame Verlagsauslieferung Göttingen GmbH&Co. KG, www.gva-verlage.de
CH: AVA Verlagsauslieferung AG, www.ava.ch
FR, BE: Interart Paris, www.interart.fr
UK: Central Books Ltd, www.centralbooks.com
US, CA, AMZ, AMS, AFR: ARTBOOK/D.A.P., www.artbook.com
KOR: The Book Society, www.thebooksociety.org
JP: twelvebooks, www.twelve-books.com
AU, NZ: Perimeter Distribution, www.perimeterdistribution.com

First edition: 2025
Printed in EU
ISBN 978-3-95905-749-3

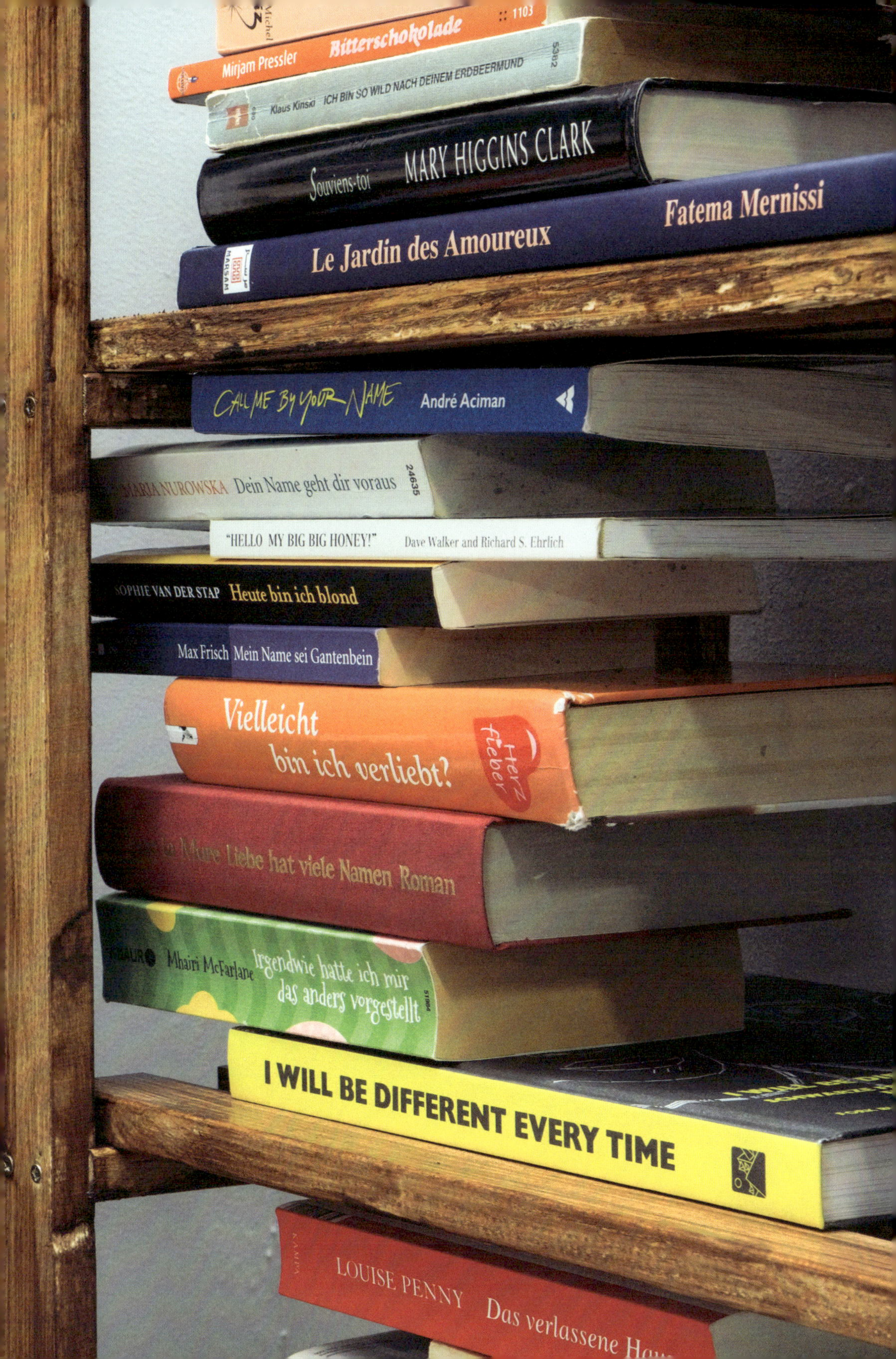

Mirjam Pressler
Bitterschokolade
1103
Klaus Kinski
ICH BIN SO WILD NACH DEINEM ERDBEERMUND
5362
Souviens-toi
MARY HIGGINS CLARK
Le Jardin des Amoureux
Fatema Mernissi
CALL ME BY YOUR NAME
André Aciman
MARIA NUROWSKA
Dein Name geht dir voraus
24635
"HELLO MY BIG BIG HONEY!"
Dave Walker and Richard S. Ehrlich
SOPHIE VAN DER STAP
Heute bin ich blond
Max Frisch
Mein Name sei Gantenbein
Vielleicht bin ich verliebt?
Herz fieber
Liebe hat viele Namen Roman
Mhairi McFarlane
Irgendwie hatte ich mir das anders vorgestellt
I WILL BE DIFFERENT EVERY TIME
LOUISE PENNY
Das verlassene

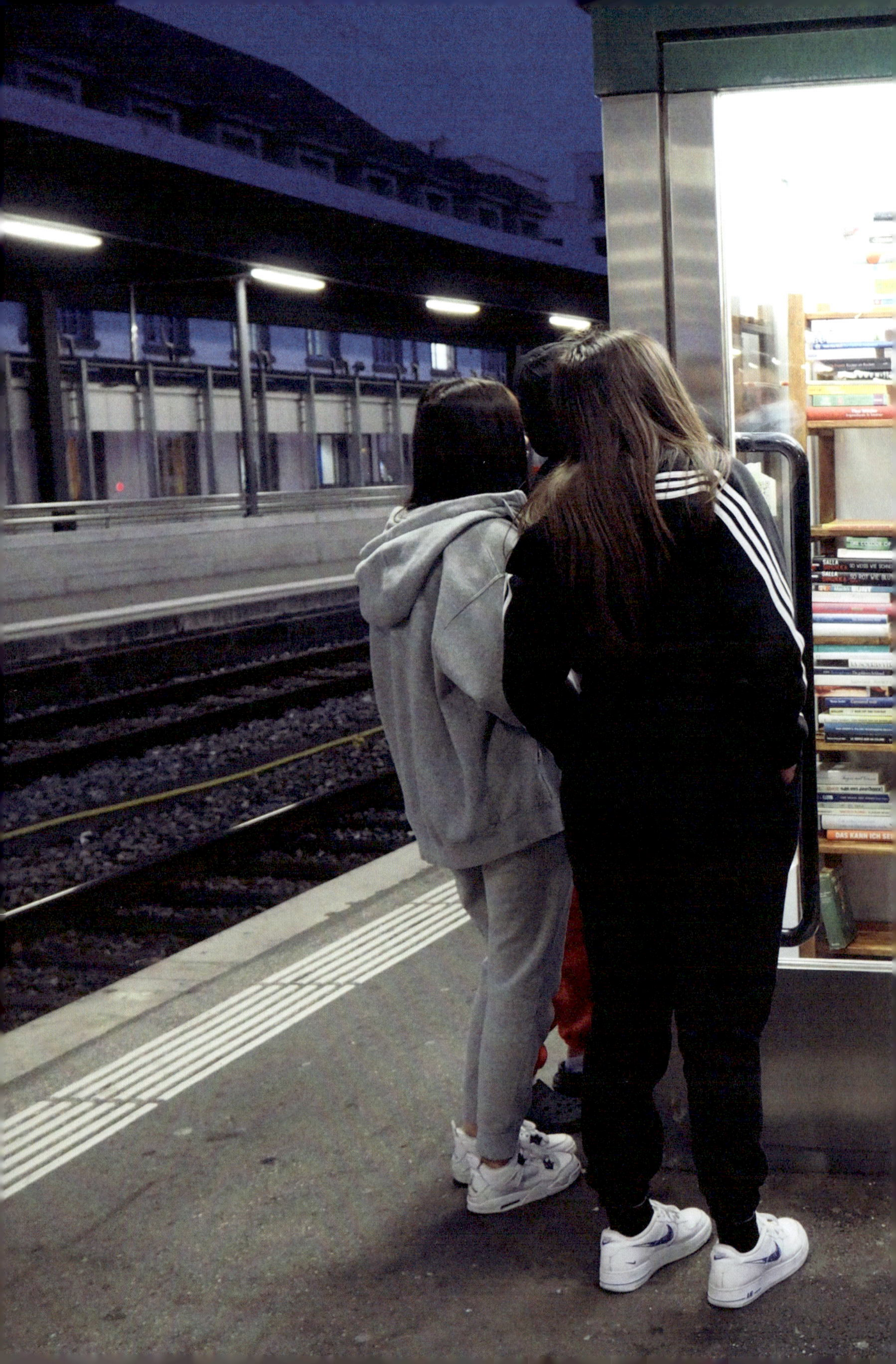
SALLA
SALLA